Karen,

Walk close to Jesus. Enjoy your journey through the New Testament!

"For the word of God is alive and active."
Hebrews 4:12

Wanda Playtn

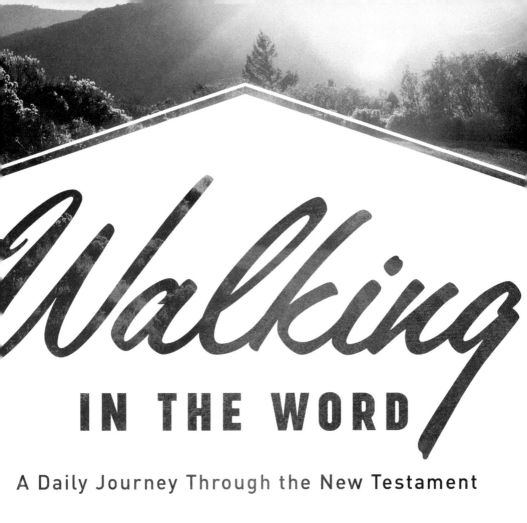

Walking

IN THE WORD

A Daily Journey Through the New Testament

WANDA PLAYTER

Beaver's Pond
PRESS

To my children:

Seth, Ben, and Hannah

I love you so much. There are so many things to learn when you're growing up. I'm proud of the young adults you're becoming. You all have unique
personalities and interests. I love that! You're busy with school, sports,
jobs, and other activities. But always remember to take time for God.

 I wrote this devotion book to help you read through the New Testament in a year. I jotted down some thoughts I want to share with you. This
will take only a few minutes every day, but the knowledge you'll gain will
last a lifetime. It's a good read. The best. Enjoy it!

All my love forever,

ISBN 13: 978-1-59298-870-9
Library of Congress Catalog Number: 2015906402
Printed in the United States of America
First Printing: 2015
19 18 17 16 15   5 4 3 2 1

Book design and typesetting by Dan Pitts.

Beaver's Pond Press
7108 Ohms Lane
Edina, MN 55439–2129
(952) 829-8818
www.BeaversPondPress.com

BEAVER'S
POND
PRESS

Reseller discounts available.

Thank you for your interest in *Walking in the Word: A Daily Journey through the New Testament*. Savor every minute as you embark on your journey through the New Testament. I use the ***New Living Translation*** as my source because it's easy to read. You can use any translation you are comfortable with.

My prayer is that you make ***Walking in the Word*** your own. Choose a designated time to read your devotion every day. If you're a morning person, begin your day in God's word. Or if you enjoy quiet time before bed, what a great way to unwind at the end your day.

As you work through ***Walking in the Word*** and the New Testament, take time to record your thoughts and concerns, or just journal about what's happening in your life that day. You're making tomorrow's memories today.

You can also read through ***Walking in the Word*** as a family or group. Take a few minutes after dinner or breakfast to read together and share what you've written in your book during the week. Some of my favorite childhood memories were around my grandparents' table. After our meals, Grandpa would read from the Bible, and then we'd sing and dance around the room. Take time to linger at the table reading God's word and to sing and dance!

This book is very personal to me. My prayer is that it will become very personal to you and your family as well.

God's Blessings,

Wanda

Matthew 1:1–2:12

Jesus is born! God chose a wonderful woman, Mary, to be his mother. God chose a wonderful man, Joseph, to be his father. God puts families together. He chose your mom and dad for you. And when the time is right, he will choose someone special for you to share the rest of your life with too. You're important to him—listen to what he has to say to you!

If these exact words were written to Jerry. I'm guessing he might wonder what to do with it. Did God really plan for Les and I to be parents of Jerry and Joe? That may be a good question. A second good question might be, "How can I be of help to Jerry at this time of life? I am not speaking of giving him money. He thinks of that as help - but I know I don't have enough money to give him what he thinks he wants.

DAY 1

Matthew 2:13–3:6

John the Baptist's message was, "Turn from your sins and turn to God, because the Kingdom of Heaven is near." Is that how you're living your life today? It's never too late to ask forgiveness for your sins and to start living for Jesus. The time to live for Jesus is *now*!

If it is a sin to "be troubled by many things" — to be tense and nervous about fitting in enough reading and studying for the groups I belong to, to be concentrating on what I don't know about using the computer for e-mailing or being secretary for Delta Kappa Gamma — then I need to work hard to bring more calm to our home. Calmness may indeed be the beginning of the Kingdom of God.

DAY 2

Matthew 3:7–4:11

It was important for Jesus to be baptized by John the Baptist. This made God happy. Think about your own special baptism day. Your sins were washed away, and you became part of God's family. This made God happy. In this passage, we also see that Jesus was tempted in the wilderness. Each time he was tempted or questioned, he responded with scripture. Because he knew what the Bible says, he knew how to react and how to handle difficult situations. The Bible prepares you for so much. Read it often!

The Bible includes advice for people in all situations. The people in the Bible were not so different from people of our time. There were people like Sara & Hannah who had not had children until late in life and there were people who tried to get by without following the plans God had. So we continue being willful and too independent for our own good.

DAY 3

Matthew 4:12–25

When Jesus called his disciples, they left everything right away, no questions asked, to follow him. Because they chose to follow Jesus, they were able to help many people. There are still many people in the world today hurting and searching for something. The something they need is Jesus. And Jesus is calling you to be his disciple, to share his love with them. Let Jesus's love show in all you do and say.

I guess the real question is "What would Jesus do?" While I was at my I-phone class tonight, Kym called and left a message for me to call her. When we had finished our supper of chow mein — Warren reluctantly told me about her call. When I called her she told me she was going to stay with her auntie because her heat had been shut off. She said Jerry was now in Crow Wing County Jail and was hungry — so would I please send him $60.⁰⁰

Matthew 5:1-26

God has blessed you in so many ways. He provides all your needs and many of your wants as well. You are so blessed! So, how can you be a blessing to someone else today? Let your light shine for all to see. Hide it under a bushel? *No*! I'm gonna let it shine, let it shine, let it shine . . .

I am not at all sure how my own light shines through this. But I am thinking I have reached my limit of wanting to give him money. It has begun to feel like what started as a gift meant to help Jerry and his kids has begun to be a danger to my finances and a detriment to his need to be responsible for his own actions. Maybe the best way for me to let my light shine is to return to Al anon principles.

Matthew 5:27-48

Jesus talks about the important commitment of marriage. Do not enter into it lightly. It's one of the most important decisions of your life. Marriage is for always. Jesus also says to be kind to others. Pray for people you have a hard time getting along with and those who make you angry. You will be amazed by the power of prayer.

I have been very fortunate in the almost 22 years I have been married to Warren. He is kind and considerate and has always been able to forgive me when I have not been as thoughtful as I should be.

I need to pray for wisdom to handle the situations that arise with Jerry. Recently he was in Hubbard County Jail and was there long enough to get about $200 from me and now he wants money

sent to Crow Wing County.

Matthew 6:1-24

When praying or serving God in any way, make sure you do it for the glory of God and not to draw attention to yourself. Don't blow your own horn: "Look at me—what a good person I am. I pray every day for sixty minutes." Or "I help do this." Or "I did that." Give God all the glory through you.

Warren and I worked at Bistro today. We went in at 1:30 and started with making pumpkin bars and the frosting that went with it. When that was done we helped with things like poking the potatoes for their time in the oven. After we ate supper we went back and helped serve the food because the servers hadn't had their supper. Dottie Hammer somehow got us some ham pieces. I've got beans soaking. I will try to get soup made tomorrow.

Matthew 6:25–7:14

It's easy to say, "Don't worry." God commands that you not be consumed with worry. Instead, put that effort into serving God. Be kind to everyone, and they'll be kind to you. And always remember to pray. Keep asking and knocking.

I led the discussion at the Bethel Women's study group today. We had read the last two chapters of Anne LaMott's book Small Victories. Thankfully people contributed to the discussion. I had been reminded of the various self help groups such as Al Anon and Emotions Anonymous and made a copy of one of the pages near the back. "Just for Today" with different endings to the sentences helped me be calmer today.

Grow and become a healthy tree. Produce good fruits pleasing
to him. Be wise. Listen to Jesus's teaching and obey him.
Study God's word and be amazed at his teachings.
Build your life on the solid rock of Jesus Christ!

after the circuit training
class was done today I tried
to relax more than I have been
the last several days. I completed
the bean soup that I put in
the pressure cooker crock pot.
We ate it tonight and the
beans were cooked well. They
had been soaked overnight and
then cooked all day and that is a
method I'd like to use again.
I finished the first draft of the
Pi Chapter minutes and sent them
to key people to proof read.

DAY 9

Matthew 8:1–17

Through faith in Jesus, all things are possible.
He can heal sick and hurting people.
Believe in him and the power he possesses.

I watched some tv tonight downstairs.
One show I watched for a while
was about the number of people
in county jails that are addicted
to alcohol or the many different
drugs that people are addicted
to. It was not very encouraging
as it relates to Jerry and the
other people in his situation.
We have to set our clocks back
an hour tonight. I have
been gentle on myself today.
I did things I felt like
doing and I rested quite a lot.

Matthew 8:18-34

Even the wind and waves obey him. Wow—what power!
Many people were frightened by it. You should embrace it.

We were at Myrna Luehmann's house today for an Acts dinner. We picked up Alan Reichart at church just after we sang the prelude for the 2nd service on this All Saints Day of 2015. We drove the route prescribed by the AAA driving directions. Alyce Nelson was on the road with her car and a police car was there too. We stopped and Alyce Said "I'm okay - tell Myrna I'll be late." The front passenger door, the rear passenger door & the rear panel will all have to be replaced. Our time together was enjoyable.

Matthew 9:1–17

Jesus came to earth to save lost sinners such as you.
He spent time with and loved the people the world looked down
on. Jesus can heal a hurting heart. He loves you and wants you
to be one of his followers. He doesn't care about your past.
He cares about your future. Follow him!

I went to Circuit training Class and
then on to the Weight Watcher
meeting at St Olaf. I was down
a few ounces which made me
happy. I have eaten too much
this afternoon & evening. It
was nice to come home to Chili
made in the Crock pot that
doubles as a pressure Cooker. I
got the minutes of the DKG
meeting sent off and had to
resend the one to Linda Lubben.

There are so many lost and lonely people in the world. Pray that Jesus will show you how to reach them. You know a lot of people. The best way to witness to them is to let Jesus's love show through you in all you do and say.

[help sleep]

Chamomile tea

Salmon   2 servings other fish

Kiwi - seratonin

tart cherry juice

edamame

jasmine rice

whole grains

Kale

Getting a good nights sleep can help me be a far better help to anyone I will spend time with.

Matthew 10:1-23

Don't be afraid to talk about Jesus.
He will give you the right words to say.
"It will be the Spirit of your Father speaking through you."

Jerry called tonight. He was asking about what Hubbard County was doing about the money he had on account. During our conversation there was a voice that interrupted and said the call would be ending in a few seconds.

I worked on reminder calls for the blood bank today. Things seemed to be going okay and then I started getting cancellations. Doug Norvald called late to say he was going to

DAY 14

come and try to give.

In this time of uncertainty and strife, what a wonderful passage to focus on. You don't need to be afraid or worry about your physical well-being. It's far more important to concentrate on your relationship with Jesus. He can't wait to introduce you to his Father, who is waiting for you in heaven.

We were not able to set the room up for the blood drive tomorrow. They were having a coloring session in one half of the room and the other half of the room was being used for a meeting of some sort so we will have double lifting and double the fun tomorrow. Jerry Gehler said he was going to bring a table mover. Maybe it will work!

DAY 15

Matthew 11:7–30

Don't find yourself thinking you're too wise for Jesus.
No matter how much schooling or how many years you study
the Bible, you will never know everything about Jesus and his
glory. Never lose your childlike faith. And when you are grown
and have children of your own, enjoy and learn from their faith.
I know I've learned a lot from my children's faith.

_____

_____

_____

_____

_____

_____

_____

_____

_____

_____

_____

Matthew 12:1-21

Jesus: "The hope of the world." Remember to keep the Sabbath, which is Sunday. Set it aside as a day of worship, rest, and enjoying others. Work hard six days a week, then take Sunday to go to church and rest from your busy week. Sunday is a day to concentrate on godly things, not worldly things.

_____

_____

_____

_____

_____

_____

_____

_____

_____

_____

_____

Matthew 12:22-45

What comes out of your mouth? The words you choose say so much about you. Do not swear or use the Lord's name in vain. There is no place for language like that. "For whatever is in your heart determines what you say." Those are bold words. Is Jesus in your heart? Others will know by the language you use.

Matthew 12:46–13:23

My prayer for you is that your roots of faith run very deep.
Open your eyes to see and your ears to hear all that God has to
offer you today and always.

Matthew 13:24-46

Heaven is the most wonderful place! Far better than we can even imagine. Think of your most favorite place. Got it? Okay. Now, heaven is way better than that. We're going to have a great time there!

_____

_____

_____

_____

_____

_____

_____

_____

_____

_____

_____

Matthew 13:47–14:12

John the Baptist prepared the way for Jesus.
That was God's plan for John's life. It didn't have a happy
ending. Sometimes bad things happen to God's people.
But God has a reason or plan we may not always understand.
Have faith in God and the plan he has for you.

_____

_____

_____

_____

_____

_____

_____

_____

_____

_____

_____

_____

DAY 21

Matthew 14:13–36

Jesus performed many miracles while he was on earth. He is still performing miracles today. Keep your eyes and heart open to them. Have faith in Jesus and his plan for you, and you won't sink. Because with Jesus walking beside you, you'll be walking on water!

Matthew 15:1–28

For one day—twenty-four hours—concentrate more on what you put in your heart than what you put in your stomach. You eat three meals a day plus snacks. Spend at least that much time in prayer and Bible study. Can you do it?

_____

_____

_____

_____

_____

_____

_____

_____

_____

_____

_____

_____

_____

Matthew 15:29–16:12

Jesus is the one who provided for all your needs. Look at all you have. Is there anything you **need** that Jesus has not provided for you? Thank him for that. This passage also tells us to beware of false teachings. Still today, people try to turn us from Jesus. Don't listen to them. Instead, hold fast in your love for Jesus, your provider.

DAY 24

Matthew 16:13–17:9

Many things will happen in your lifetime. Many you will question. God has a reason for everything. He has a perfect plan for your life. He is preparing you for heaven. It's hard for us to see with our human eyes and to understand with our human minds. Trust in God, and soon you'll be talking to Moses and Elijah!

Matthew 17:10-27

How great is your faith? Look at a mustard seed. It's so small,
only a speck. And with a speck of faith, mountains can be
moved. Nothing is impossible! Remember that with faith in God,
you can do anything. Don't ever doubt that truth.

_____

_____

_____

_____

_____

_____

_____

_____

_____

_____

_____

_____

Matthew 18:1–20

Children are so important. Jesus tells us many times how important children are. Always treat them with respect and love. Relationships too are so important. Remember to always put people before possessions. How much better is it to have a great friend than to have a great car? I would choose a friend over a car any day!

Matthew 18:21–19:12

When you forgive someone, it counts only if you forgive with your heart. Saying "I'm sorry" or "I forgive you" isn't enough. You have to mean it and say it from your heart. God forgives us over and over. You need to do the same for others. Don't ever hold a grudge. It will eat away at you. Jesus also talks about marriage and divorce again. Marriage is forever. It's a huge, but wonderful, commitment. It's a relationship you'll have to work hard at but is one of the most rewarding.

_____

_____

_____

_____

_____

_____

_____

_____

_____

_____

DAY 28

Matthew 19:13–30

How do you get to heaven? Not by being important or having lots of money. The only way is through Christ Jesus. Only by faith and believing in him can you be saved. It is only by the grace of God. You cannot work your way to heaven. Your good works come because of your love for Jesus.

DAY 29

Matthew 20:1–28

Don't worry if you're not treated fairly or not given your fair share. God is a fair God. He knows all. You will receive your just reward in heaven. He has a spot ready for you. How much greater your reward will be in heaven than it could ever be on earth?

Matthew 20:29–21:22

Hosanna! Jesus, the Son of God, riding humbly on a donkey.
How awesome it would have been to be there and be able to
put your coat or palm branches on the ground for Jesus.
Also read verse 22 again. Prayer is a powerful thing—use it!

_____

_____

_____

_____

_____

_____

_____

_____

_____

_____

_____

_____

_____

DAY 31

Matthew 21:23-46

Jesus is the cornerstone! He is our rock, our foundation on which we build our homes and lives. He was sent by his Father to teach us. What have you learned by the example Jesus set?

_____

_____

_____

_____

_____

_____

_____

_____

_____

_____

_____

_____

_____

Matthew 22:1–33

You have been invited to the greatest party ever! Will you accept the invitation? Will you be too busy to attend? Don't get so wrapped up in earthly parties that you miss the best party of all—*heaven*.

Matthew 22:34–23:12

Notice the commandments Jesus says are the most important. They both deal with love. *Love* the Lord your God, and *love* your neighbor. If you truly love God and others, everything else will fall into place.

_____

_____

_____

_____

_____

_____

_____

_____

_____

_____

_____

_____

Matthew 23:13–39

I wish I could keep my children protected under my wing forever. But I can't. They have to live their lives. They will have many choices to make. You will too. Make those choices wisely. Don't make choices as the Pharisees do, just to look good and holy to others. God knows what is in your heart. And he knows the motives behind the choices you make.

Matthew 24:1–28

We are seeing signs of Jesus's return today. Wars and
earthquakes. Things will get worse before they get better.
Keep your faith. Be patient. Jesus is coming!

_____

_____

_____

_____

_____

_____

_____

_____

_____

_____

_____

_____

Matthew 24:29–51

Stay alert. No one knows when Jesus is coming again.
You cannot take a vacation from God. Don't get so wrapped up
in partying and having a good time that you forget Jesus.
He needs to be number one in your life, always.

Matthew 25:1–30

God has given you many treasures and talents. How are you investing yours? Don't be afraid or ashamed of them. Don't bury them. Instead, use your money and talents to glorify God. You can't out-give God. Just try—I dare you!

_____

_____

_____

_____

_____

_____

_____

_____

_____

_____

_____

_____

Matthew 25:31–26:13

Always help those in need. Don't ridicule or look down on others. You may need help one day too. Instead, give them what they need—food, water, clothing, friendship. When you do that, God's love will be seen in your actions. Also, 26:6–13 tells a favorite story my daughter, Hannah, remembers from kindergarten Sunday school. The woman worked one whole year to pay for the perfume she used to wash Jesus's feet. Would you give up a year's wages for him?

Matthew 26:14-46

The first communion. When you take communion at church, it's like participating in the Last Supper with Jesus. He tells you to stay alert and pray. He tells you this because he knows temptations will be great and the only way to get through them is with God's help.

Matthew 26:47-68

What a difficult thing for Jesus to have to go through. He knew before he came to earth what he would have to endure here. He was fulfilling prophecy—what was predicted in the Old Testament. Still, Jesus loved you so much that he was willing to go through all the suffering for you. That is the greatest love of all!

Matthew 26:69–27:14

Have you ever denied Jesus? It's much easier to follow the crowd than to stand up for Jesus. If you can't act like a Christian around a group of friends, then those friends are not worth hanging around. Be proud you are a Christian, and know Jesus as your personal Lord and Savior!

_____

_____

_____

_____

_____

_____

_____

_____

_____

_____

_____

DAY 42

Matthew 27:15–31

Today's verses are one of the saddest and hardest parts
of the Bible. The people had so much hate in their hearts.
They were blinded by it. But we know the outcome. Their hate
was no match for God's love. Read on and see . . .

_____

_____

_____

_____

_____

_____

_____

_____

_____

_____

_____

_____

_____

_____

_____

DAY 43

Matthew 27:32–66

"Truly this was the Son of God." Even the Roman officers and soldiers knew it was true after seeing the signs. One of my favorite signs was when the curtain in the temple was torn from top to bottom. Only God could have started that tear. What awesome power and signs for all people to see.

Matthew 28:1–20

He arose! Oh, to see Jesus! What wonderful words he left with us: "I am with you always, even to the end of the age." You have nothing to fear, for Jesus is with you at all times. But (there is always a "but") He also left a large task for you: to tell everyone about Jesus. Remember, he will be with you while you carry out this task. Congratulations—you have made it through your first chapter!

Mark 1:1–28

There is no question as to who Jesus was: "Jesus the Messiah, the Son of God." Even the evil spirits knew him and called him "the Holy One sent from God." A great way to worship and praise Jesus is to make a list of names used to describe him. The names from these verses can be at the top of your list.

Mark 1:29–2:12

Jesus told his disciples they must go to other towns because that is the reason he came to earth—to teach and save people. Not just the people who lived in one area. Not just people of one race. Not just people who spoke a certain language. He came to save *all* people, including you and me. He is counting on us to finish that job for him.

_____

_____

_____

_____

_____

_____

_____

_____

_____

_____

_____

_____

_____

Mark 2:13–3:6

Jesus, the Son of Man (add that name to your list), is the master of the Sabbath. The Sabbath was made to benefit the people. The people were not made to benefit the Sabbath. Enjoy Sunday. It is a great day for relaxing and enjoying family and friends. Work hard all week—then take time to enjoy the special day God has made for you.

Mark 3:7-30

People were crowding around Jesus. They wanted just to see him, just to touch his gown to be healed. We have Jesus with us always. We can call on him in prayer at any time of the day. His awesome power has not changed from when he was alive on this earth. Now he is alive in heaven, waiting for you to call on him. Seek him with the same passion as the early believers.

Mark 3:31–4:25

It's important to pay attention and listen with an open mind to Jesus's teachings. He has so much to teach you. Let his light shine and let his fruits grow in fertile soil.

_____

_____

_____

_____

_____

_____

_____

_____

_____

_____

_____

_____

_____

Mark 4:26–5:20

Thank Jesus for sharing parables with us. His teachings and knowledge are so great that you could never comprehend it. Thank him for putting his teachings into stories you can understand. In his awesome wisdom, he knows just how much to reveal to us.

Mark 5:21–43

"The Teacher" is another name for Jesus. Being a teacher is an incredible job. Teachers mold the minds of their students. Jesus was the ultimate teacher. He came to teach us how to live and to save us from sin. He was able to help so many people. If you have faith, he will help you too!

Mark 6:1–29

This is a horrible story about how John the Baptist died. Remember, life isn't always fair. John was a good man, but because of an evil woman, he died. It sounds awful. But today John is happier than ever living in heaven with his friend Jesus.

_____

_____

_____

_____

_____

_____

_____

_____

_____

_____

_____

Mark 6:30–56

Jesus performed many miracles while he was on earth. He would not let people leave hungry. When you have guests in your home, be hospitable. Don't let anyone leave hungry for food—or hungry for the word of God. Be a holy host!

_____

_____

_____

_____

_____

_____

_____

_____

_____

_____

_____

_____

_____

Mark 7:1–23

Traditions are good. We enjoy the comforting feeling we get from traditions and their familiarity. But don't be so set in tradition that you are afraid of change. Keep your focus on what is pleasing to God.

_____

_____

_____

_____

_____

_____

_____

_____

_____

_____

_____

_____

_____

Mark 7:24–8:10

What a wonderful time on earth when Jesus was here.
He healed so many people. He fed so many people. Not only
with food for the body but with food for the soul. He is still
feeding you today, if you just take the time to be quiet and listen
to him. Eat it up until you are full and your cup runs over!

Mark 8:11–38

"Who do people say I am?" Jesus asked his disciples.
Who do people say *you* are? When they were small, my children
were known as "Mike and Wanda's kids." As they have grown,
they've formed their own identities. When people hear *your*
name, what do they think of? Who do they say *you* are?

_____

_____

_____

_____

_____

_____

_____

_____

_____

_____

_____

_____

Mark 9:1-29

When Jesus came down from the mountain, he found his
disciples arguing. Don't argue, especially with your family.
Treat each other with respect and love. You're family!
And remember, "anything is possible if a person believes."
Ask God to help you "not to doubt."

Mark 9:30–10:12

Jesus talks to his disciples again about the importance of living in peace with one another. What kind of Christian example are you if you can't get along with your own siblings? Jesus loves children! They're so important. Don't look down on them but treat them with respect. And finally, Jesus talks about marriage again. Once you're married, it's forever. You're no longer two people dating, but one. Your dreams and goals need to be one also. Talk about these things before you decide who you'll spend the rest of your life with. Marriage is the most wonderful thing when you get to share your life with the one you love. Be patient. God will give you that person. I know, because he gave me the perfect husband to share my life with.

Mark 10:13–31

Always keep your childlike faith. As you grow older,
don't get all wrapped up in having things. God's view of wealth
and importance is very different than the world's view of wealth
and importance. Who are you trying to impress with your things?

_____

_____

_____

_____

_____

_____

_____

_____

_____

_____

_____

Mark 10:32-52

Remember you are to serve others, not to be served.
Don't think of yourself as being better than anyone else.
Whoever is first will be last, and those who are last will be first.
God is preparing a place for you in heaven now!

Mark 11:1–26

Wow—what a trip for Jesus's disciples. They went to so many towns and saw so many people. And Jesus taught them so much. But guess what? Jesus is teaching you too. The disciples wrote down what Jesus taught them so you could know his teachings too. How great is that? And today Jesus is telling you that if you come to him with a clean heart, he will answer your prayers. Talk to Jesus. He wants to have a relationship with you like he had with his disciples.

Mark 11:27–12:17

Jesus is not impressed by money. You can't buy your way into heaven. He tells the Pharisees to pay what they owe. You should do the same. If you owe people money, pay them. Don't overextend yourself by spending more money than you have. Remember to pay the church and Jesus first. Then pay your bills.
I read once that the definition of *wealth* was "consistently having money left over every month after paying your bills."

Mark 12:18–37

Love—fill your heart with love, and everything else will fall in place. Love God with your whole heart. Now Jesus tells you to love your neighbors as much as you love yourself. He doesn't say to love the people in your class, or to love the people in your hometown, or to love the people in America, or even to love all the people with the same skin color as you. No! You are to truly love **all** people, even those who have hurt you.

Mark 12:38–13:13

If the end of time was near and people were being persecuted for being Christian, would you be singled out as a follower of Christ? When people at school or work see you, do they know you are a Christian? *And they will know we are Christians by our love, by our love. Yes, they will know we are Christians by our love.*

Mark 13:14–37

The end times sound scary. But stay strong in Christ Jesus. ***Onward, Christian soldier!*** He will get you through those difficult days. But what an ending—what a reward—to see Jesus and his angels come down from heaven to take us home with them. Wow! I will meet you in the clouds!

Mark 14:1–21

Jesus knows everything. There is nothing you can hide from him. He knows everything you do and everywhere you go. He even knows all the thoughts you think. He knows you better than you know yourself. Trust him!

_____

_____

_____

_____

_____

_____

_____

_____

_____

_____

_____

_____

_____

Mark 14:22-52

When Jesus was praying to God, his Father, he prayed that God's will be done. God is your Father as well. He has a plan for your life. Trust him when you pray. And pray that God's will be done in your life. When God closes a door in your life—watch for the window he opens!

Mark 14:53–72

You can be a strong Christian only with God's help. Even Peter,
Jesus's faithful disciple, denied knowing him.
Ask God to give you courage and strength to stand up for him.
You can do nothing apart from God.

_____

_____

_____

_____

_____

_____

_____

_____

_____

_____

_____

_____

_____

Mark 15:1–47

Jesus went through all that pain, suffering, and torture for me and you. People treated him so badly. He came to earth to help and save people. Instead, they killed him. That is how great Jesus's love is for you—that he was willing to endure all that pain so you can spend eternity with him in heaven.

Mark 16:1–20

Jesus is alive! You don't need to be afraid of death anymore, because now you know that death is your doorway to heaven. In God's timing, when you have completed your portion of his work on earth, he will take you to be with him in heaven. Then you will hear these words: "Well done, my faithful servant."

Luke 1:1–25

"My words will certainly come true at the proper time," the angel Gabriel said. Sometimes it's hard to live on God's timeline. It's hard to be patient when you want things or answers now. Believe in God and his perfect timing!

Luke 1:26–56

What blessed women. There's nothing more exciting than having a child. How exciting it must have been for Mary and Elizabeth, knowing the impact their sons would have on the world. God chose Mary (a servant girl) and Elizabeth (a woman too old to have children) to carry out his divine plan! How will he use you?

_____

_____

_____

_____

_____

_____

_____

_____

_____

_____

_____

DAY 73

Luke 1:57–80

When my children were born, we celebrated their births as a
family. They were also celebrated throughout the neighborhood!
They had an extended family of neighbors who loved them.
The hand of the Lord was upon you at your birth too.
His guiding hand has never left you. Let him lead you as
you continue to walk with him.

_____

_____

_____

_____

_____

_____

_____

_____

_____

_____

_____

Luke 2:1–35

Jesus is born! The shepherds were busy watching their flock, doing their shepherd thing, when an angel came to them, announcing the Savior—yes, the Messiah, the Lord—had been born that night in Bethlehem. Now, the shepherds could have said, "Great. Whatever. Let's get back to work." But no. Instead, they *ran* to the village and found Mary and Joseph—and the baby lying in the manger. What will you do when you hear God calling? Will you say, "Whatever. Let's get back to work"? Or will you *run* to his call?

_____

_____

_____

_____

_____

_____

_____

_____

_____

Luke 2:36-52

There's no such thing as luck. God has a plan. He had a plan for Baby Jesus growing up, and he has a plan for you growing up too. It's not luck that you were born into your family. *No.* It was God's plan for you. Believe in God, not luck or other superstitions.

Luke 3:1–22

John the Baptist told people to put their faith into action.
They asked what they should do. John gave them direction
about what actions to take. Don't just talk about your faith,
but *do* something because of your faith.

_____

_____

_____

_____

_____

_____

_____

_____

_____

_____

_____

_____

_____

_____

_____

DAY 77

Luke 3:23–38

Today we learned a history lesson: from Jesus all the way back
to Adam and God, with Noah, Abraham, and Isaac included.
What a family tree! How far back can you trace your family tree?

Luke 4:1–30

The devil tempted Jesus. You'll be tempted many times in your life. Knowing what the Bible says and knowing what Jesus taught will greatly help you overcome those temptations. Also, beware of men twisting the words in the Bible or taking them out of context to tempt you. Stay close to Jesus. He will show you the way out.

Luke 4:31–5:11

Our God is an awesome God! What power and authority Jesus
had. People were in awe of him. The demons obeyed him.
Fishermen left everything to follow him, to become fishers
of men. He teaches so much to those who will listen.

_____

_____

_____

_____

_____

_____

_____

_____

_____

_____

_____

_____

Luke 5:12–28

As Jesus's life got busier and busier, he often went away by himself to pray. Your life will get busy too. Remember that quiet time is important. Turn off the TV or music, and pray. Listen quietly to what God has to say to *you*.

_____

_____

_____

_____

_____

_____

_____

_____

_____

_____

_____

_____

_____

Luke 5:29–6:11

Jesus is master of the Sabbath. It's a day to do good deeds, not for doing harm. Think of a good deed you can do this Sunday. Remember that little things count too.

Luke 6:12–38

Read this passage again. It tells you so much about how
you should treat others. Live by these words.
Be loving, kind, and gracious.

_____

_____

_____

_____

_____

_____

_____

_____

_____

_____

_____

Luke 6:39–7:10

Don't judge others. Don't spend so much time worrying about what your friends or siblings are doing wrong that you don't see that you yourself have many sins in your life. Produce good deeds. Speak well of others.

Luke 7:11-35

Life is not a game. Jesus spent his life healing people physically and spiritually. Jesus was perfect, yet people criticized him. People will surely criticize you. Live your life to please Christ. Because no matter how hard you try, you'll never please all people. You'll find peace only in living for Christ.

Luke 7:36–8:3

Jesus forgives all your sins. How do you show your gratitude to him? Don't hold back; he deserves your all!

_____

_____

_____

_____

_____

_____

_____

_____

_____

_____

_____

_____

_____

Luke 8:4–21

You have seen God's work, but do you *really* see?
You have heard God's words, but do you *really* understand?
Let your lamp shine for all to see!

_____

_____

_____

_____

_____

_____

_____

_____

_____

_____

_____

_____

_____

Luke 8:22-39

Jesus instructed the man who had been possessed by a demon to tell his family and friends all the wonderful things God had done for him. You're supposed to do the same. Make a list of all the wonderful things God has done for you. Now share that list with your family and friends.

Luke 8:40–9:6

Oh, the power of Jesus! Just by touching the fringe of his robe, people were healed. Just think how much he will do for you, his child with whom he has a close, loving relationship.

Luke 9:7–27

Jesus still has the same requirements for his followers today:
Put aside selfish ambition.
Shoulder your cross daily.
Follow him.

_____

_____

_____

_____

_____

_____

_____

_____

_____

_____

_____

_____

_____

Luke 9:28-50

Prayer was very important to Jesus. He spent much of his time on earth praying to his Father in heaven. God is your Father too! How much of your time are you spending talking to your Father in heaven?

_____

_____

_____

_____

_____

_____

_____

_____

_____

_____

_____

_____

_____

DAY 91

Luke 9:51–10:12

Jesus expects you to be his disciples. He is calling you and me
to spread his love to others. Don't look back—just look forward
at what you can do for the Kingdom of God.

Luke 10:13-37

The disciples were privileged to see firsthand Jesus's power at work. You also are privileged to have the Bible, which documents Jesus's life. Read it over and over. God is speaking to you through it. What a privilege to be a child of God!

Luke 10:38–11:13

Jesus teaches us how to pray:
Keep on asking.
Keep on looking.
Keep on knocking.
Jesus will take care of you!

Luke 11:14-36

You should strive to have a pure eye to let sunlight flood your soul. Be filled with light so your whole life will be radiant with God's love shining through you.

Luke 11:37–12:7

Jesus was angry with the Pharisees. They were so worried about "cleaning on the outside." They were concerned about their outward appearance and thought they were better than everyone else. Jesus says what's important is what's on the inside—in your heart. Don't forget to look around you and help those who need it.

Luke 12:8-34

Verse 15 means: "Don't be greedy for what you don't have. Real life is not measured by how much we own." Wow! It isn't a contest to see who has the biggest house, fastest car, or most toys. God gives you many blessings and gifts. How will you use yours?

_____

_____

_____

_____

_____

_____

_____

_____

_____

_____

_____

_____

Luke 12:35–59

Are you ready? God has given you many gifts. Much more is required from those who have been given much. Rejoice in your abilities, and use them to glorify God.

Luke 13:1–21

You can always find shelter in God's branches—his arms.
If you're ever feeling sad or alone, remember that God is always
waiting for his children. Let him hold you in his branches.

Luke 13:22–14:6

Which of the prophets are you most excited to meet in heaven? Or maybe it is a Christian singer you want to sing with in the angel choir. Or a pastor. Or a teacher. You will have time to do it all because we will be there for eternity!

Luke 14:7–35

Jesus tells you that in order to follow him, you must give up everything. By doing so, you show your true faith to him. He will provide everything you could ever need. Trust him!

_____

_____

_____

_____

_____

_____

_____

_____

_____

_____

_____

_____

_____

Luke 15:1-32

Rejoice over every found lamb. Be happy and celebrate with anyone who has been lost in sin and is now found.

Luke 16:1–18

Who is your master? Money can be an evil thing. Always put God before money. And always use your money to help others by making their lives easier.

_____

_____

_____

_____

_____

_____

_____

_____

_____

_____

_____

_____

Luke 16:19–17:10

Take care of business. Do your duty. Obey the Lord. Don't expect praise or glory for any works you do. You're simply doing what is expected of you.

Luke 17:11–37

Keep watch, listen, and be prepared for when Jesus comes back for you and me. Don't cling to the things of this world but instead turn and run straight to Jesus. He will be waiting for you with open arms.

Luke 18:1-17

We have all sinned. We all need forgiveness. Pray and repent
often. Humbly come before God, and he will hear your prayer.

_____

_____

_____

_____

_____

_____

_____

_____

_____

_____

_____

_____

_____

_____

_____

_____

_____

Luke 18:18–43

Maybe you have gone to Sunday school for years.
Maybe you know the Bible stories and the Ten Commandments.
Maybe you know the right answers to Bible questions. All of that
alone will not get you into heaven. You need to have faith in God,
and he needs to be number one in your life,
above all others and all things.

Luke 19:1-27

God has given you riches and talents. How are you using what God has given you to improve his kingdom? Can you be trusted with much, or only a little?

_____

_____

_____

_____

_____

_____

_____

_____

_____

_____

_____

_____

_____

_____

Luke 19:28-48

What a wonderful song of praise: "Bless the King who comes in the name of the Lord! Peace in heaven and glory in the highest heaven." Keep a song of praise in your heart at all times. The Psalms are full of them. If God's people don't sing them, the stones will.

Luke 20:1-26

Jesus is your cornerstone. On Jesus, the cornerstone, you need to build your live. He is the foundation. He was so wise and not influenced by what others thought.

_____

_____

_____

_____

_____

_____

_____

_____

_____

_____

_____

_____

_____

_____

DAY 110

Luke 20:27-47

Jesus promised life after death. You will be like an angel, living in heaven with him and Abraham and Isaac and Jacob.

_____

_____

_____

_____

_____

_____

_____

_____

_____

_____

_____

_____

_____

DAY 111

Luke 21:1–28

Stand strong in difficult times. Know that God is with you.
He will be on your side, helping you through every painful step.

Luke 21:29–22:13

Every day Jesus went to the Temple to teach. It is important for you to study and learn from God's word, the Bible, every day. Spend time with Jesus learning, listening, and praying. Do it every day.

Luke 22:14–34

Jesus shared the Last Supper with his disciples. Now you can share it at church with your Christian brothers and sisters. Don't take communion lightly. Remember what it symbolizes. Remember all Jesus endured here on earth for you and for me. His body and his blood.

Luke 22:35–53

"Pray that you will not be overtaken by temptation." There are temptations everywhere you look. You cannot do the right thing without God's help. Pray for strength and wisdom so you're not overtaken by temptation.

Luke 22:54–23:12

It breaks my heart to see Jesus treated cruelly. It also breaks my heart to see young people treat other young people cruelly. Don't do it—don't be a bully! Be a friend and treat others with love and respect.

Luke 23:13-43

What suffering and pain Jesus endured for you. That's how much he loves you. He was willing to go through it all so you could be saved and spend eternity in paradise with him.

Luke 23:44–24:12

Jesus has risen from the dead! We serve a living God!
Even death has no power over him.
He is almighty!

_____

_____

_____

_____

_____

_____

_____

_____

_____

_____

_____

_____

_____

_____

Luke 24:13-53

"There is forgiveness of sins for all who turn to me,"
Jesus said. Just as Jesus was with the two men from Emmaus
and with his disciples, he is with you also. He has sent the
Holy Spirit to fill you with power.

John 1:1–28

What do you think of when you hear "the Word"? Do you think of the Bible? In today's passage, "the Word" *is* God. It has been here since the beginning. Nothing exists that he didn't make. Wow! Think about everything you have. It's all from God!

_____

_____

_____

_____

_____

_____

_____

_____

_____

_____

_____

_____

John 1:29-51

You have been baptized with water, and the Holy Spirit has descended upon you. He is now living in you because you are God's special child. No matter where you go in this world, he is with you.

_____

_____

_____

_____

_____

_____

_____

_____

_____

_____

_____

_____

John 2:1–25

Turning water into wine. When Jesus's mother asked for his help, he answered, "My time has not yet come." God knows when **your** "time has come." Willingly answer him, "Yes, Lord." You are never too young (or too old) to serve for God. Let him use you.

_____

_____

_____

_____

_____

_____

_____

_____

_____

_____

_____

DAY 122

John 3:1–21

Do all things in the light! Everyone knows John 3:16, but the following verse, 3:17, is just as powerful. Memorize it too. God did not send his Son into the world to condemn it but to save it.

John 3:22–4:3

John the Baptist tells you that God in heaven appoints each person's work. This is not just your career path. But also the work you do in the church and the work you do for God's kingdom. God has given you special talents to carry out his work. Put those talents to good use.

John 4:4–42

Jesus, who was born a Jew, took time to talk and witness to a Samaritan woman. Jesus's example shows us that you need to tell everyone about Jesus. People from every country, every race, and every gender. Make time for all people.

John 4:43–54

Jesus gave us many miraculous signs while he was on earth. The people needed only to believe. That is what he still asks of us today. Do you believe in him? With your whole heart? Above anything else? Jesus loves you.

John 5:1–23

Thank you, God, for sending your Son, Jesus, to earth to live with us. Being a Christian means you're "Christlike." You can learn so much from the examples Jesus gave you. Follow God the Father with your heart and with your life.

_____

_____

_____

_____

_____

_____

_____

_____

_____

_____

_____

_____

John 5:24–47

Be careful of whom you trust. Be careful of whom you honor.
Are you honoring God—or man (famous people) or even yourself? God needs to be at the top of your list. To God be all honor
and glory. Amen.

John 6:1–21

Life is a journey. Jesus makes the journey so much easier. Keep Jesus close in the good times and bad. Jesus always has the answers and a way out of any trouble. Just listen and trust him. He feeds thousands of hungry people and calms the water. He will care for you too!

John 6:22-42

Memorize verse 35: "I am the bread of life. No one who comes to me will ever be hungry again. Those who believe in me will never thirst." Follow Jesus for the right reasons. Not to please your mom and dad. Not to receive a pastor's blessing. Not to get things from Jesus. When you truly believe in Jesus, he will take away your hunger and fill that void as only he can. Let him fill you to overflowing!

John 6:43-71

What a neat image of communion. When you go up for communion, you're not just eating a chunk of bread and a tiny glass of wine. No, you are taking Jesus's flesh and blood into your body. How awesome is that? You can be that intimate with your God. Jesus came to earth so you could have that intimacy with him. What a sacrifice he made for you and me.

John 7:1–30

In verse 7, Jesus said the world hated him because he accused it of sin and evil. There will be times when people of this world will hate you too. They won't understand your beliefs. They won't understand when you value people over power or value morals over money. Stick to your beliefs. Some may ridicule you, but always know Jesus is with you and smiling at your choices.

John 7:31–53

Feelings were mixed about Jesus. Some believed him, while others despised him. That's still true today. Although we know and love Jesus, some people don't. It's hard for us to fathom why anyone wouldn't open their heart and life to Jesus. He is such a loving God. Those people must be so lonely. Let them see Jesus's love through you.

John 8:1–20

We have all sinned—moms, dads, grandmas, grandpas, and kids. We have *all* sinned. So be very careful not to judge others. Don't be pointing fingers at other people. Instead, focus on helping others and doing good with your life.

John 8:21-30

Jesus is still, today, the one he has always claimed to be. In this world of change and quick fixes, isn't it nice to know Jesus never changes? God the Father is true. God never deserted or left Jesus. They were always together, always one. You are one with Jesus too. He is living in your heart, he will be with you always, and he will never leave you.

John 8:31–59

Who's your daddy? There are only two fathers: the father of sin (the devil) and the Heavenly Father (God). Which father do you want to follow? It's your choice. If you're living in sin, you're not following God. Your Father, God, is standing with his arms wide open, waiting for you to run to him.

John 9:1–41

Jesus looks at things so differently than we do. Consider how he views this man's "disability" in verse 3: "He was born this way so the power of God could be seen in him." How do you treat people with disabilities? They should not be shunned but celebrated. Next time you're feeling sorry for yourself because of some little physical problem (maybe you have acne, or you're a slow runner, or you're feeling fat), remember to rejoice in the body God has given you. May his glory be seen through it.

John 10:1–21

Jesus, Lamb of God—worthy is your name! Oh, the story of the Good Shepherd. I love this imagery of Jesus as the loving, caring shepherd. Let Jesus shepherd you. Listen to him. Let him lead you. He knows where the wolves are and how to keep you safe from them.

John 10:22-42

Blasphemy—the act of expressing lack of reverence for God. Isn't it ironic that Jesus was put to death for blasphemy? *Blasphemy*? Of all things, lack of reverence for God? Jesus was perfect. But the world can be so full of sin, so evil, even to a perfect man who came to save them. So when the world and people seem cruel to you, remember that Jesus has been through it too. Talk to him. He has been through the same thing, and his heart aches for you. Soon you will be home in heaven with him and leave this evil world behind.

John 11:1–54

Jesus does things in his time. Mary and Martha were frantic. Their brother, Lazarus, was sick and near death. They needed Jesus to come *now*. But what did Jesus do? He waited. Jesus went later so God would receive glory. I think waiting is one of the hardest things to do. When I pray, I want God to hit me on the head with either a yes or a no. Hearing God say "wait" is much harder to deal with. However, I'm beginning to realize God has a reason for his "wait" answers. I have learned patience—which, yes, is a virtue. My biggest and hardest "wait" prayer was when my husband and I decided we were ready and wanted to have a baby. God said, "Wait." We got pregnant with Seth two years later. Two years of praying hard, two years of God saying, "Wait. You're not ready yet." We prayed for another year to get pregnant with Ben. And then even more prayers before we got our angel, Hannah.

John 11:55–12:19

Look how Mary cared for Jesus by washing his dusty, dirty feet with very, very expensive perfume. You can learn a couple things from Mary here. First, to have a servant's heart that cares for others. Second, to give Jesus the best you have. Don't give him the cheap leftovers of our time, talents, or gifts. Give him your best.

John 12:20–50

Be children of the light (verse 36). Don't be like the Jewish leaders who loved human praise more than the praise of God (verse 43). Instead put your trust in the one who has come as a light to shine in the dark world (verse 46). It's much easier to find your way through an unknown area when you have a light. Keep Christ's light shining bright in your life, and he will lead your way.

_____

_____

_____

_____

_____

_____

_____

_____

_____

_____

_____

_____

John 13:1–30

Jesus came to be an example for us. He is *Jesus*, and what did he do when he came to earth? He became a servant. Don't ever think you're "too good" to do servant work for others. Jesus did the dirtiest, worst job there was—he washed feet. Follow Jesus's example. Be a servant to someone today.

_____

_____

_____

_____

_____

_____

_____

_____

_____

_____

_____

_____

_____

_____

_____

_____

John 13:31–14:14

Jesus has given you a new commandment. "The Great Commandment"—to love each other. It sounds so easy. By being a kind, loving person, others will see Jesus's love through you. Jesus finishes this passage by telling you that his life on earth may be over, but he is still very much with you. Jesus went to heaven to be with his Father. He tells you to ask anything in his name and he will do it. He is waiting to hear from you. He is still very present today in your everyday life.

John 14:15-31

Jesus came to earth for just a short time. He did many great things and taught many valuable lessons. When Jesus left to be with his Father again, he left you a gift and a promise. The gift is the Holy Spirit. The promise is that Jesus is coming back to take you to heaven to live with him and his Father.

John 15:1–27

Are you producing fruit that will last? If you're connected to the vine—Jesus—he will produce mature, beautiful fruits from your branches. Once God has produced the fruits, share them. If your fruit just sits on the vine, it will rot. Nothing is sadder to God than to see his beautiful fruit withering, unused and rotting on the vine.

John 16:1–33

You are never alone. Even when your parents or loved ones can't be with you, Jesus always is. He knows you'll have sadness in your life. He knows you'll have struggles. He knows you'll have to make some tough choices. He will always be with you. Jesus has come and overcome the world. He is with you. You have nothing to fear.

John 17:1–26

In this entire passage, Jesus is praying for you! How awesome is that? He is praying to his Father, God, to keep you safe in this world full of evil and danger. He loves you that much.

_____

_____

_____

_____

_____

_____

_____

_____

_____

_____

_____

_____

_____

John 18:1–24

Verse 4: Jesus fully realized all that was going to happen to him. Still he went. Still he suffered and died, for you. In verse 11, Jesus replies, "Shall I not drink from the cup the Father has given me?" Again, Jesus knew his fate. Still he went. The Old Testament scriptures were being fulfilled.

John 18:25–19:22

Pilate was working hard to free Jesus, but the people wouldn't hear of it. They wanted Jesus crucified. So, during this sad story, where was God? Jesus was his one and only Son. How awful it must have been for God to watch people treating his Son so badly. Yet God let it be done. He loves you so much that he let the abuse continue. God was looking beyond the cross. He was looking at today, when his child—you—would be reading his word, the Bible, and spending time with him.

John 19:23–42

Now Jesus knows he is dying and will soon be in heaven with his Father. But as he is hanging there, he looks down to see his mother and aunt. His heart goes out to his mother, and he asks his disciples to care for her. It was important to Jesus that after he left this world, his mother would be taken care of.
Family matters to Jesus.

John 20:1–31

Are you like Thomas—doubting? Don't be. Jesus says, "Don't be faithless any longer. Blessed are those who haven't seen me and believe anyway." You haven't seen Jesus yet, but someday soon when you're in heaven with him, you'll see with your own eyes his hands and pierced side. Oh, what an amazing day that will be!

John 21:1–25

Jesus tells Peter to feed and care for his sheep. You are one of Jesus's sheep. Jesus instructs Peter to tell you about him. When he was here on earth, Jesus did so many wonderful things; if everything were written down, the whole world couldn't hold all the books. And he was here for only thirty-three years. Just think of it. He is still doing wonderful things.

Acts 1:1–26

And now you begin Acts. It's important to learn all you can about Jesus, God, and the Holy Spirit, allowing your faith to mature. But remember, there are many things so great about God that our little minds cannot comprehend them. That is where faith comes in. Believe! The Holy Spirit fills that gap between your brain and heart.

Acts 2:1–47

God has given you and me the gift of the Holy Spirit. And because the Spirit lives in us, we're able to do great and wonderful things for Jesus. The Holy Spirit enables you to serve God and to share the Good News of Jesus with others here on earth.

Acts 3:1–26

There are things on earth worth more than money can buy. The lame beggar asked Peter and John for money. They had no money. What they did have was better! They had Jesus, and they were able to heal this man. No amount of money could be better than that. Thank Jesus daily for all the gifts he has given you. What value can you put on health, family, and friends? Jesus gives them all to you. Praise him!

Acts 4:1–37

Peter and John were ordinary men who had received no special training. Yet God used them. They were filled with the Holy Spirit, who gave them courage and the words to speak boldly. Because of their willingness, many believed in Jesus. God uses ordinary men and women to make an extraordinary difference in the world.

Acts 5:1–42

Do not lie. At the beginning of today's passage, you see what happened to Ananias and his wife, Sapphira. They schemed a perfect lie. Guess what? It didn't work. It never does. Even if you can scheme and lie to other people and get away with it, God knows. He knows you. He knows your intent. He knows your heart. So be careful. Live an honest life, and fill your heart with good things.

Acts 6:1–15

There are many "good" things you can do with your life.
But every so often, you need to step back and evaluate whether
you're truly doing what God has called you to do. Are you feeding
the masses and getting lost in busy work? Or are you sharing
the Good News of Jesus, spreading his word? God has given you
special gifts and talents. Use them to glorify him!

Acts 7:1–29

God does great things with ordinary people. You may not see the fruits of your labor today or tomorrow or for four generations (four hundred years). But God has a plan and is at work. Are you willing to open your heart and let him work through you?

Acts 7:30–50

Verse 43: What is your real interest? Is it God? Or is it a man-made idol, such as gold, money, a career, or a house? They are all made by human hands from gifts God has given you. They are all good things, but don't miss God's greatest gift to you—his Son, Jesus!

Acts 7:51–8:13

Sorcery and magic are only illusions. They are not the real deal. Even Simon knew that. Great things and miracles only happen through the power of Jesus. What miracles have you seen in your own life lately?

Acts 8:14–40

Simon asked to buy the Holy Spirit in verse 18. This gift cannot be bought. It cannot be earned. It's a gift from God while you're on this earth. The Holy Spirit lives in your heart and will guide and protect you from the sins of this world. What an awesome help God has given you.

Acts 9:1–25

God works through some of the strangest people. You never know when or where he will use *you*. Just think, if he can use Saul, who hated Jesus and anyone who believed in him, what might he have planned for you? So you can listen and follow, or he can knock you over the head to get you to listen! Either way, it's important to listen to what God has planned for your life.

_____

_____

_____

_____

_____

_____

_____

_____

_____

_____

_____

Acts 9:26–43

Traveling missionaries. Even just after Jesus died, people were traveling to faraway lands, spreading the Good News of Jesus Christ and helping those in need. The same things are happening today. But you don't need to be a full-time missionary to spread the Good News or to help those in need. There are many opportunities right where you live. How can you help someone in need today, and in doing so, spread Jesus's love?

Acts 10:1–23

Prayer is so important. Verse 2: Cornelius was a man who prayed regularly. Verse 9: Peter went up to the flat roof to pray. Talk to Jesus daily. Tell him your concerns, your problems, and your joys. Then take time to listen to what he has to say to you. Praise God for his wonderful direct line of communication. Prayer changes things. It changes lives. Spend some extra time in prayer today.

Acts 10:24–48

In verse 34, Peter tells us that God doesn't show partiality. He accepts all who love and respect him. It doesn't matter what state or country you're from. It doesn't matter if you're a boy or girl. It doesn't matter what color your skin is or what language you speak. God loves you! So if God loves all people, then you too should love your brothers and sisters in Christ, regardless of race, nationality, or language.

Acts 11:1–30

Great things happen when you let God lead you. Keep your ears open, your eyes open, and, mostly, your heart open to what God is doing for you and around you. God has great things planned for your life! Let him guide and lead you.

Acts 12:1–23

There will always be bad people. There will always be people who don't know Jesus and try to make others hate him too. But God is stronger than any of them. He has defeated Satan and will defeat any evil power of this world. All things are possible when you believe in Jesus. PS: See verse 5–the Church prayed *very earnestly* for Peter.

Acts 12:24–13:15

No one can stand in the way of God's work. Not even an evil sorcerer with his bag of tricks. God's love will prevail!

_____

_____

_____

_____

_____

_____

_____

_____

_____

_____

_____

_____

_____

_____

_____

Acts 13:16–41

Verse 20 says God took 450 years to fulfill his promise to the people of Israel. That's 450 years! We become impatient when we have to wait an hour, a day, a week, or one year for God's answer. How about 450 years? Now look ahead to verse 39: "Everyone who believes in Jesus is freed from all guilt and declared right with God." What a wonderful promise. Just turn it all over to Jesus.

_____

_____

_____

_____

_____

_____

_____

_____

_____

_____

_____

_____

Acts 13:42–14:7

Paul and Barnabas preached the Good News of Jesus in many towns. Many people believed in Jesus because of their teaching. In 13:43, they tell the people, "By God's grace, remain faithful." Even when people of this world tell you that you're crazy for being a Christian, "By God's grace, remain faithful."

Acts 14:8–28

When Paul, or any one of Jesus's followers, tells you in a loud voice, "Stand up!"–do it. Don't hesitate. Don't be afraid. Do it. Have faith to stand up for Jesus. In verse 17, what has Jesus sent you lately to remind you of his love? Rain, good crop, food, joyful heart.

Acts 15:1–35

God loves people. He loves Jews and Gentiles, boys and girls, white skin and brown skin. He loves people who know and love him. Do you do the same? Do you love all people regardless of nationality, sex, or race? Don't judge others. Instead, love others!

Acts 15:36–16:15

What incredible faith Paul and Silas had! God gave Paul a vision
at night, and Paul decided to leave right away in the morning to
help people in need in another country. "They left at once." How
many times have you felt God calling you to do his work, but you
pushed it aside? But God keeps prodding, nudging. Wouldn't it
be easier to follow Paul's example and "leave at once"
to do God's will?

Acts 16:16–40

People of this world have a hard time understanding God's ways and values. They only understand worldly values and what and who is important here on earth. Live beyond this world. Live for Jesus! What can you do for Jesus today? Stand up for Jesus. Let someone today know how important Jesus is to you. Live today with God's values, not man's values.

Acts 17:1–34

After Jesus died, Paul spent his days traveling to tell people everywhere about Jesus. What a ministry! He didn't sugarcoat his message. He told it like it is. People listened. Some believed, and some did not. But Paul continued telling Jesus's story without worrying about his safety or whether people would "like" him for what he was saying. Paul had one focus, one passion: to tell as many people as he could about Jesus so they would come to know the one true God.

Acts 18:1-22

Paul was a busy and determined man. He knows he was called to share the Good News of Jesus. He traveled and worked hard telling everyone he met about Jesus. He didn't care what others believed or what religion they were. Paul knew that Jesus was the only true God, and he let people know it.

_____

_____

_____

_____

_____

_____

_____

_____

_____

_____

Acts 18:23–19:12

Thank God for people like Apollos, Priscilla and Aquila—and for
Paul, who told others about Jesus every day. What persistence!
Verse 7 states that twelve men were saved. Not an auditorium of
a thousand but twelve. There is great rejoicing and celebrating
in heaven when even one is saved. Tell the story of Jesus to just
one. Make a difference in that person's life. God bless you and
give you wisdom and strength to be a "Paul" in today's world,
telling others the Good News of Jesus.

Acts 19:13–41

Be careful—be very careful. Stay grounded in Jesus. Don't get caught up in the little grumbles or riots that people cause. Stay focused on the Word.

Acts 20:1–38

Paul's entire journey was led by the Holy Spirit. Paul worked hard to care for God's people. He didn't want for a fancy house or clothes or an expensive car. What an example. "My life is worth nothing unless I use it for doing the work assigned me by the Lord Jesus—the work of telling others the Good News about God's wonderful kindness and love." This is Paul's final message as he leaves Asia to head to Jerusalem. It is for them, and you, to be sure you feed and shepherd God's flock—his church.

Acts 21:1–17

Wow! What a trip! Paul continues to travel for Jesus. Try to map out Paul's journey. Some of the names have changed. But just imagine traveling in Paul's day, with no cars, no buses, no air-planes, no motels, or no restaurants. It was not an easy vacation full of sight-seeing. He worked hard and suffered so that others would come to know Jesus's love!

Acts 21:18–36

People (even Christians) do not do well with change. I pray that you study God's word, the Bible. Know its content. Do not follow man; follow God. Do not follow tradition; follow God. Be wise. Spend time in God's word and listen to what it has to say to you.

Acts 21:37–22:16

God has a plan for you and your life. If you listen closely, he will whisper it to you. If you can't hear him at first, don't worry. Some people need to be blinded by a bright light to hear what God is telling them. Keep your eyes and heart open, and God will make known his plan for you.

Acts 22:17–23:10

Paul was a smart man, but just a man. God gave him the courage and wisdom to face the high priest and the crowds against him. May God give you the same courage and wisdom when you are up against people who question your religious beliefs.

_____

_____

_____

_____

_____

_____

_____

_____

_____

_____

_____

_____

_____

_____

Acts 23:11–35

Today we read about another leg of Paul's journey. God is still leading and protecting Paul. God is keeping his faithful servant safe, even though there are men plotting to kill Paul. *My God is so big. So strong and so mighty. There's nothing my God cannot do, for you!*

_____

_____

_____

_____

_____

_____

_____

_____

_____

_____

_____

_____

_____

Acts 24:1–27

Praise God for Paul—the "ringleader" for Jesus. Oh, if only more people were accused of being the same! Paul was on trial because he believed in Jesus's resurrection from the dead. He was kept in prison for two years. The entire time, he witnessed to Felix, the governor. We are on trial every day for Jesus. Do you defend him, or deny him?

Acts 25:1-27

Paul makes the Jewish people uneasy. They accuse him of many untrue things. But Paul never compromises his belief in Jesus. He stands firm, even as the men close in around him at his trial to kill him. Paul still shares the Good News of Jesus.

Acts 26:1-32

Reread verse 6. Are you like Paul? Are you looking forward to the fulfillment of God's promise made to your ancestors? Do you hope for Jesus to come back to earth to take you to live with him in heaven? Oh, what a day that will be! I will meet you there!

Acts 27:1-20

Even with God in your life, you will go through storms. The true test of being a Christian is how you travel through those storms. Sunnier days will follow. So if you find yourself in the eye of the storm, hold close to Jesus. Only he is the light that will lead you to brighter days.

Acts 27:21-44

An angel came to Paul in the night to encourage him to not be afraid. Listen to the angel. You, my child, have nothing to be afraid of. God loves you so much. He knows your needs and will protect you. So do not be afraid of anything. Listen to the angel.

Acts 28:1–31

Paul went on quite a mission trip! But now he has returned to his home. He continues to tell everyone about Jesus. No matter where in the world you are, people need to hear about Jesus. Not only on mission trips in other parts of the world. Those who live and work with you every day also need to hear the Good News of Jesus's love.

Romans 1:1–17

Today we begin exploring a new chapter—Romans, written by Paul. Paul, in the **New Living Translation** I'm reading, is referred to as Jesus Christ's "slave." How does that make you feel—to be a slave for Jesus? Are you too proud to be a slave? Humble yourself. Live a simple life pleasing to God. Live your life being a slave to Jesus Christ!

Romans 1:18-32

God has put the knowledge of what is wicked and sinful in your hearts. Do not give in to wicked and evil ways. Instead, live a pure life in the fear and love of God. Worship him, the Creator, not what he has created. His creation is for your enjoyment, but it was never meant to be worshipped.

Romans 2:1–24

Do not judge others. Concentrate on your personal relationship with God and on sharing his love with others. Show love, not judgment, to others. God will do the rest! Plant love in the lives of others, and watch God grow it into maturity.

_____

_____

_____

_____

_____

_____

_____

_____

_____

_____

_____

_____

_____

_____

Romans 2:25–3:8

Doing and saying all the right things is not important. What is important is having your heart in the right place. When you love Jesus with your whole heart, then you will do and say all the right things for all the right reasons.

_____

_____

_____

_____

_____

_____

_____

_____

_____

_____

_____

_____

_____

Romans 3:9–31

Thank you, God, for sending your Son, Jesus to save us. There's no way we could be diligent enough to follow all the Old Testament laws. We could never work hard enough to make our way into God's grace. No, the only bridge to God is belief in his Son, Jesus Christ. Thank you, God, for sending your Son!

Romans 4:1–12

All of the ceremonies we have in church—such as confirmation and recognitions for Sunday school and youth group—are good. They are great opportunities to share your faith with others. But what is way more important is your personal relationship with Jesus. When your heart is right with Jesus, and you are walking closely with him, the ceremonies at church have much more meaning.

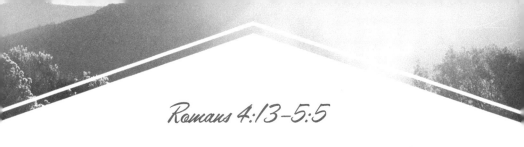

Romans 4:13–5:5

Praise God! When you're having a bad day, reread 5:1–5. How can those verses not change your negative attitude? You have been made right in God's sight; you have peace with God. Christ has brought you into this place of highest privilege. And as the verses explain, your problems and trials are good for you. Lean on Jesus and his Word when you are discouraged. God will speak to you just as he spoke to Abraham. Then all you have to do is believe in God's promises the way Abraham did.

Romans 5:6–21

Today's reading starts, "When we were utterly helpless . . ." Have you ever felt utterly helpless? I think we've all had days like that. Some days it's hard to be optimistic or happy about anything. But the Bible says to rejoice in your wonderful new relationship with God, all because of what the Lord Jesus Christ has done for you in making you a friend of God. So when you feel helpless and the world is treating you harshly, remember that you have a friend in God. You can take all your cares to him. He wants to hear about your joys too.

Romans 6:1-23

You are no longer a slave to sin. Do not put your focus on "not sinning"—it's almost impossible. Instead, put your focus on Jesus and his righteousness. Then it'll be much easier to do the right thing and resist sin. Put your mind on what is pure and lovely. Trust God. Focus on Jesus, and he will guide you through the tough times.

Romans 7:1–13

Sin and Satan are truly terrible. They take what is good and twist it for their gain. If sin can twist God's law, just think how it can twist our lives. That's why it's so important to stay connected every day to Christ, who has power over sin and Satan.

Romans 7:14–8:8

Even Paul wrestled with a sinful nature. The only way to overcome it is through the Holy Spirit—by placing your faith and
trust in Jesus Christ. Because he died for my sins, I have hope.
I may still face daily struggles to do the right thing, but because
of Jesus's strength, he overcomes my weakness.

Romans 8:9–25

You are a child of God—hallelujah! You have been adopted into his family. Because your Father loves you so much, he wants to spend time with you in heaven. He has sent the Holy Spirit to live in you and guide you while you're here on earth in your mortal body. God gives us hope for today of great things he has planned for you and for me. Hallelujah!

Romans 8:26–39

Amen! You are so blessed to be loved by God! So unworthy,
but so blessed. He knows your heart better than you do.
We can be so fickle. But not God. He is all-knowing and always
near whenever you need him. When you're feeling lonely, know
that God is close by, wrapping his arms of love around you.
Fall into his embrace.

_____

_____

_____

_____

_____

_____

_____

_____

_____

_____

_____

_____

DAY 205

Romans 9:1–24

We're saved through the grace of God, not by works. There's nothing you can do to "earn" God's love. You're blessed because God has chosen you to be his child. What you do with that gift is up to you. Be a willing vessel for God to display his love through you.

Romans 9:25–10:13

Praise God! You do not have any hoops to jump through, any tests to pass to prove you're a Christian. You could never be strong enough or smart enough to measure up on your own. No, you just need faith. Believe in your heart, and confess with your mouth. And praise God, you are his child!

Romans 10:14–11:12

Verse 15–"How beautiful are the feet of those who bring good news." No wonder Jesus and his disciples wore sandals. They had beautiful feet! How do your feet look? Is it time for a spiritual pedicure? Do *you* have beautiful feet?

_____

_____

_____

_____

_____

_____

_____

_____

_____

_____

_____

Romans 11:13–36

Verse 33–"Oh, what a wonderful God we have! How great are his riches and wisdom and knowledge! How impossible it is for us to understand his decisions and his methods!" What a comforting verse. You don't need to worry about anything because you have a wonderful, wise, knowledgeable God who loves you and wants only the best for you, his child. Put your trust and faith in him, and don't worry about the small stuff.

Romans 12:1-21

Today's reading is my prayer for you. Read it again and again
and again. These verses describe how to live! Not conforming
to this world's measures. But to live for God. Always giving your
best of the gifts he has blessed you with!

Romans 13:1–14

Obey the government laws. God is the one who put those laws in place. Even when you disagree, remember God gave us rules for a reason. Live within the law, and you have nothing to fear. Let the Lord Jesus Christ take control.

_____

_____

_____

_____

_____

_____

_____

_____

_____

_____

_____

_____

_____

_____

_____

_____

Romans 14:1–23

Here's another passage about loving one another. Be kind and loving to others, especially other Christians. Do not judge them. Concentrate on your actions instead of theirs. Live a life of goodness and peace and joy in the Holy Spirit.

Romans 15:1–22

Life is not supposed to be lived alone. We are to live in community with others, in complete harmony and love. If you're ever feeling down, reread verse 13. I pray that God will keep you happy and full of peace as you believe in him— and may you overflow with hope.

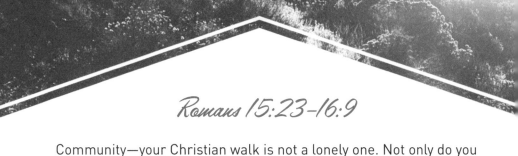

Romans 15:23–16:9

Community—your Christian walk is not a lonely one. Not only do you have Christ by your side and the Holy Spirit in your heart, you have an entire community of believers on the same path as you. Encourage each other. Especially the ones becoming weary. A kind word or small gesture is exactly what they need. When you become weary, remember to lean on your community. You are not alone.

Romans 16:10–27

Paul sends greetings to quite a long list of people. Take a few minutes to compile your own list of fellow Christians who have strengthened your faith. Now make another list of fellow Christians you have helped strengthen their faith walk. Are you content with your lists? Can you think of anyone you would like to add to your second list? What's stopping you? Make a difference in that person's faith life today!

1 Corinthians 1:1–17

Paul's message to the church in Corinth is to stop arguing amongst themselves. Instead of doing Christ's work, they spend their time arguing about small things. Don't get caught in that trap. The devil would love nothing more than to get you off track so you aren't being fruitful doing God's will. Stay focused on God's big picture for your life, and do not get wrapped up in petty arguments. Follow Christ. Not man or pastor or church, but God.

1 Corinthians 1:18–2:5

We are all smart. Don't become so arrogant that you think you're wiser than other Christians or wise enough to know all there is to know about God. Communicate Christ's message to others so they can understand it and be saved. Remember your purpose is to glorify God, not yourself by using large words in long speeches. Serve with a humble and loving heart.

1 Corinthians 2:6–3:4

Thank you, God, for sending the Holy Spirit to live in me and to help me to understand your ways, not the world's. Continue to grow in your faith. Do not live as a Christian infant your entire life. Strive for more than milk. The solid food is amazing!

1 Corinthians 3:5-23

What medium are you building with? Whatever medium you choose, make sure it will last. Also, be sure whatever you build fits on the foundation of Jesus Christ. And be ready for the next builder to come along to add the next layer. Because no solid structure can be built by one man or woman.

1 Corinthians 4:1–21

What would you be willing to give up for Jesus? He has blessed you with all that you have. So why do you hold on to it so tightly? Don't let your earthly possessions keep you from following Christ. If you are talking the talk, you better be walking the walk 100 percent. Your actions speak so loudly that no one will hear what you're saying.

1 Corinthians 5:1–13

This is a hard passage for me to read. Paul tells us that as Christians we need to hold other Christians accountable for their actions. It's much easier to look the other way when a brother or sister in Christ is sinning. But in reality, it's your responsibility to address the issue with them. Lord give you the strength to face these issues head on, in love.

1 Corinthians 6:1-20

You are beautiful! God made you special, amazing, and unique. Honor your body. Do not abuse it. Your body is the temple of the Holy Spirit. Treat it with respect.

_____

_____

_____

_____

_____

_____

_____

_____

_____

_____

_____

_____

DAY 222

1 Corinthians 7:1–24

Relationships are not easy. They take time and devotion. Do not enter into a relationship lightly. Pray over it long and hard. As a mother, every day I pray for my children and you, that God bless you with a loving Christian spouse.

_____

_____

_____

_____

_____

_____

_____

_____

_____

_____

_____

_____

_____

DAY 223

1 Corinthians 7:25-40

Happiness or sadness or wealth should not keep anyone from doing God's work. Neither should a friend or spouse. Neither should anything from this world. So, what's stopping you from doing God's work?

_____

_____

_____

_____

_____

_____

_____

_____

_____

_____

_____

_____

_____

1 Corinthians 8:1–13

Today's reading talks about the example you need to set for other Christians. Live with love for them. Do not cause them to stumble. Do not debate or argue the small things, such as eating meat. The big picture is to love one another. Sometimes we get so wrapped up in the minutia that we lose sight of the goal: love one another.

1 Corinthians 9:1–18

Support your pastor and missionaries. Life is good when you are passionate about doing God's will. Do it not for the money or the approval of man but out of your love for Jesus. I pray you find your special way to glorify him!

1 Corinthians 9:19–10:13

Train to be a Christian as hard as you train to be an athlete before an event. Be prepared and fit for your work for Jesus. Remember that no matter how bad things seem, God is faithful and will get you through every temptation you face.

1 Corinthians 10:14–33

What kind of message does your life send to nonbelievers or even other Christians? Don't be the type who on Sunday puts on a "holy hat," goes to church, takes communion, and then worships another God the rest of the week. Do you have any idols that keep you from completely giving yourself to Jesus? If you do, it's time to remove that idol from your life.

1 Corinthians 11:1–16

God made the first woman, Eve, from man, Adam. But every man since Adam has been born from a woman. This does not make men superior to women, nor does it make women superior to men. Both boys and girls come from God. Both boys and girls are made perfectly. Both boys and girls are created to work together to glorify God.

1 Corinthians 11:17-34

Do you take communion seriously enough? It's such a special time between you and Jesus. Take the time to prepare before communion as well as time after communion to be with him. It is a holy sacrament. Do not take it for granted.

_____

_____

_____

_____

_____

_____

_____

_____

_____

_____

_____

DAY 230

1 Corinthians 12:1–26

Be part of the body! God has given you a special ability. Use your ability, no matter how big or how small, to work in conjunction with others so that as a whole, you are working together to glorify God.

_____

_____

_____

_____

_____

_____

_____

_____

_____

_____

_____

_____

_____

_____

DAY 231

1 Corinthians 12:27–13:13

Love—the greatest gift of all! Don't be stingy with your love. Give it away. When you truly love, everything else falls into place. Life is more enjoyable. You become a more beautiful person. When you love, you live the life God has called you to live. Now, go out and love somebody today!

_____

_____

_____

_____

_____

_____

_____

_____

_____

_____

_____

1 Corinthians 14:1–17

Love others. And through that love, teach them about Jesus.
Reach them where they are. Make it easy for them to understand. In doing so, they will believe it's possible to grow in their
faith. Keep it real!

_____

_____

_____

_____

_____

_____

_____

_____

_____

_____

_____

_____

1 Corinthians 14:18-40

Verse 33: "For God is not a God of disorder but of peace." We tend to get all excited and fired up at times. It's okay to be passionate, but be aware of how you share that passion and excitement. Your views will be received more easily if you share them in an orderly, peaceful manner. For that's what God desires of you.

1 Corinthians 15:1-28

What a beautiful day that will be. Praise God for sending his Son, Jesus, so he could live among us sinners, die for us sinners, come back again for us sinners so we can live in heaven with him. Praise our loving God!

_____

_____

_____

_____

_____

_____

_____

_____

_____

_____

_____

_____

_____

_____

_____

_____

1 Corinthians 15:29-58

Bad company corrupts good character. Choose your friends wisely. The passage also describes what a beautiful thing God does for us as our bodies begin wearing down. We can look forward to the new heavenly bodies he has waiting for us. I can hardly wait for that day, to see the flowers you've bloomed into. Your soul blossoms every day because God is at work in you.

1 Corinthians 16:1–24

Be generous with your money, time, and talents to help those who spread the Good News of Jesus Christ. Take the time to look in your community. There are people right in your own backyard spreading God's word. Encourage those people. And remember to do all things in love!

2 Corinthians 1:1–11

Think of a time in your life when you leaned on God. He is always there during the good times to celebrate with you. He is also there during the bad times to give you comfort. Knowing God is there for you and that he is in control will give you an inner peace nothing or no one can touch. But now you're asked to take that comfort and share it with others in need who do not know the comfort of Jesus. Show them the peace and comfort that only comes from Jesus.

2 Corinthians 1:12–2:11

Are you a man or woman of your word? Your reputation is based on it. Does "yes" mean "yes," and "no" mean "no"? Jesus never wavers between yes and no. There are no gray areas in Jesus Christ! Or as it says in Proverbs 22:1: Choose a good reputation over great riches, for being held in high esteem is better than having silver or gold.

2 Corinthians 2:12–17

"Spread the Good News like a sweet perfume." Just last night, my daughter, Hannah, walked into my studio and said it smelled so good. She wanted to know what that smell was. She came over to me and smelled the sweatshirt I had been wearing all day. "It's you, Mom. You smell so good!" I wasn't wearing any perfume. But all night she said she could smell me. And this morning I read about life-giving perfume. Praise God for the way he works in our lives! Our lives are a fragrance presented by Christ to God.

2 Corinthians 3:1–18

Do you glow with the glory of God? You've been blessed with so much. Can others see the reflection of God glowing in your face? If not, then it's time to clean out the old gunk to let the glory of God shine through you.

2 Corinthians 4:1–12

Reread today's passage, verses 8–12. These verses do not say that your life will be a fairy tale because you believe in Christ. No, quite the opposite. They say your life will be difficult, "pressed on every side by troubles." But you won't be crushed or broken because you believe in Christ. He lives in you. Then the passage goes on to say that through these troubles, you will share in Jesus's death and become more Christlike. Others will see Jesus through you. What a beautiful thing to live in a perishable container.

_____

_____

_____

_____

_____

_____

_____

_____

_____

_____

2 Corinthians 4:13–5:10

What types of things have you done with your body? What a glorious day it will be when we have new, perfect, heavenly bodies! Don't get all wrapped up in today's troubles. They will pass. Look ahead to the brighter days in the future. God has a plan for you. So enjoy the journey. Enjoy your time in your earthly body as you grow into your heavenly one.

2 Corinthians 5:11–21

"Whatever we do, it is because Christ's love controls us." Wow!
What a great faith statement! What a great way to live your life!
To know that you do what you do every day because Christ's love
is the center of your life.

_____

_____

_____

_____

_____

_____

_____

_____

_____

_____

_____

_____

_____

_____

2 Corinthians 6:1–13

Paul and his coworkers gave up everything to tell others
about Jesus. They gave up all—and still had great joy.
True happiness is not found in money or possessions.
It is found in Christ.

2 Corinthians 6:14–7:7

What type of friends do you have? Associate yourself with other Christians. Your life will be so much easier and so much more fun when you hang out with other believers. Negative people will bring you down. Optimistic, positive people will lift you up.

2 Corinthians 7:8–16

God is always teaching, always molding you. Take time to reflect on how God is using you and others in your life to help you mature into an adult Christian. Rejoice in your trials!

2 Corinthians 8:1–15

Give as the churches give in Macedonia—give happily and will-ingly to those in need. Christ became poor so that you could be rich. You cannot out-give God. Share your love, your talents, and your dollars with those who need it. You'll be a happier, more content person when you do.

_____

_____

_____

_____

_____

_____

_____

_____

_____

_____

_____

2 Corinthians 8:16–24

You have been given the generous gift also! What will you do with the gift God has given you? Will you be an honorable witness, like Paul or Titus? Be enthusiastic and passionate about the Lord. Praise his name wherever you go, to all people you meet.

_____

_____

_____

_____

_____

_____

_____

_____

_____

_____

_____

_____

DAY 249

2 Corinthians 9:1–15

Generosity and enthusiasm are contagious. Catch them! It's amazing how good they make you feel. Give cheerfully—not out of pressure or guilt, but with love and a grateful heart.

_____

_____

_____

_____

_____

_____

_____

_____

_____

_____

_____

_____

_____

2 Corinthians 10:1-18

Verse 17: "The person who wishes to boast should boast only of what the Lord has done." What has the Lord done for you that you can boast about? He has done *so* much for *you*. Tell others, and don't be shy to boast about the many great things the Lord has done for you. You have been blessed!

2 Corinthians 11:1–15

Do not be deceived. Be careful whom you believe. Many people disguise themselves as followers of Christ for selfish reasons—for gain of their own. Be cautious. Spend personal time alone with Christ. Study his word. Listen to what he has to say to you.

2 Corinthians 11:16–33

What have you done or given up in your life to live for Christ?
Read through the list again of everything Paul has gone through.
When you decide to live for Christ, the road is seldom easy.
Are you willing to take the road less traveled? To walk up those
hills? To tread over the bumps? If you are, you're not walking
alone. Christ is taking every step with you. He is standing right
beside you. Lean on him when the road becomes long.

_____

_____

_____

_____

_____

_____

_____

_____

_____

_____

_____

2 Corinthians 12:1–10

"My power works best in your weakness," God tells Paul. And Paul replies, "For when I am weak, I am strong." Celebrate your weakness! Celebrate God's strength! Celebrate through God's eyes, not the world's perspective.

_____

_____

_____

_____

_____

_____

_____

_____

_____

_____

_____

DAY 254

2 Corinthians 12:11-21

How would Paul feel if he came to visit you at school or work today? Would he find quarreling, jealousy, outbursts of anger, selfishness, backstabbing, gossiping, conceit, or any disorderly behavior? Paul's message is not only to the Corinthians, who lived years ago. This message is for you, today.

2 Corinthians 13:1–13

Encourage each other. Live in harmony and peace. Greet each other in Christian love. Your relationship with God is a very personal relationship, but it's meant to be shared with others. Let God's love flow through you and shower others so they too may know the love of Jesus.

Galatians 1:1–24

Live today in the grace and peace of God the Father. Don't worry about being a people pleaser. *Relax*. Enjoy the comfort of his grace and peace.

_____

_____

_____

_____

_____

_____

_____

_____

_____

_____

_____

_____

_____

_____

_____

Galatians 2:1–16

If someone were spying on you—as they were with Paul, Barnabas, and Titus—would they see your "freedom in Christ Jesus"? Freedom in Christ Jesus—just think of it . . . No boundaries, no one to please, no expectations. Just living freely in the love of Christ!

_____

_____

_____

_____

_____

_____

_____

_____

_____

_____

_____

_____

_____

DAY 258

Galatians 2:17–3:9

Verse 20 reminds me of "Temporary Home," the country song by Carrie Underwood. This earthly body you're living in is only a temporary body. Soon you'll be with Jesus in a new, glorified body. No aches, no pains—just beauty. God hasn't given you this earthly body to sit around doing nothing. Think of one thing you can do with your temporary body to glorify God.

Galatians 3:10–22

Thank you, Jesus, for your sacrifice of coming into this crazy world to save me! I fall short every day in so many ways. Yet you still love me. You were willing to endure such pain and loneliness for me. Thank you. Amen.

Galatians 3:23–4:31

The Bible was written many years ago. In verses 26–28, you're given a lesson on equality. We're all Christians—one in Christ Jesus. We're all brothers and sisters in Christ Jesus. So then love and care for others the way you love and care for your family.

Galatians 5:1–12

I think I have a new favorite Bible verse to share with you.
(Though I could say that every day!) Verse 6: "What is important
is faith expressing itself in love." Why haven't I seen this verse
on walls? It should be everywhere. I love it. My new mantra—
faith expressing itself in love! Amen.

Galatians 5:13-26

You've been given the freedom to serve one another in love! It is a gift you have been given. Some days it doesn't feel like a gift to serve others. But it is. It's a blessing to serve someone in an attitude of love. And as verses 22–23 tell you, you are given another gift. The fruits of the spirit: love, joy, peace, patience, kindness, goodness, faithfulness, gentleness, and self-control.

Galatians 6:1–18

Don't get tired of doing what's good. Don't "give till it hurts." Instead, give until the hurting stops. So many people are hurting in this world. What can you do to help ease their pain? Don't be discouraged. Continue to give in love from your heart.

Ephesians 1:1–23

May grace and peace be yours, sent to you from God our Father and Jesus Christ our Lord. The only way to find true peace and contentment is through Jesus. Praise his name for the overwhelming peace and grace he bestows on you every day. Alleluia!

Ephesians 2:1–22

You are God's masterpiece. He has created you anew in Jesus Christ so you can do the good things he planned for you long ago. A masterpiece! A priceless masterpiece. You are beautifully perfect in God's eyes—and in mine.

Ephesians 3:1–21

God has given Paul a special ministry of sharing the Good News of Christ Jesus to the Gentiles. Even though he is in prison, Paul still praises God for the blessings of his special ministry. God has given you a special ministry too. No matter what your circumstances, God can and will do amazing work through you if you are willing. Be open to his leading. What will God accomplish through you?

Ephesians 4:1–16

Today's passage begins with Paul begging you to lead a life worthy of your calling—for you have been called by God. Wow! How has God called you to live your life? What special gifts has he blessed you with? Are you using those gifts to glorify God? Through Jesus's love for you, use your gifts to love others.

Ephesians 4:17–32

Don't live like the ungodly, for they are hopeless and confused.
Their closed minds are full of darkness. But instead, live a life
filled with love and kindness. Do an honest day's work, speak
well of others, and encourage them in their faith walk.
Be a blessing to someone today!

Ephesians 5:1–33

WWJD: What Would Jesus Do? Follow his example, and live your life as Christ did. Today's passage explains with great detail how a Christian marriage should work. Young people today don't take these words to heart. They're worried about, "What's in this relationship for me?" If more couples lived their marriage the way God intended, there would be much less divorce.
Love and respect your spouse!

Ephesians 6:1–24

Work hard. Not only when your boss is looking. Work hard at all times as if you were working for Christ. How seriously do you take the work you do? No matter if it's a job or school or home-work, do you give it your all? If not, it's time to step it up. Put on the entire armor of God, and get after it. No matter what your circumstance, be the best Christian you can be!

_____

_____

_____

_____

_____

_____

_____

_____

_____

_____

_____

_____

Philippians 1:1–26

Be bold for Christ! Even in prison chains, Paul continues to praise God. He finds ways to share his faith with others. Instead of throwing a pity party for himself, Paul rejoices for the opportunities he has been given to share the Good News of Jesus.

Philippians 1:27–2:18

Humble yourself in everything you do. Stay away from complaining and arguing. A day spent helping others is a good day. Far better than a day dwelling on your circumstances. No matter what, there's always someone you could help or encourage. Whose day will you brighten today? Let Christ's love shine through your fingertips.

Philippians 2:19–3:3

Do you have anyone in your life like Paul, Timothy, or Epaphroditus? Someone who gives so that you and others may know the love of Jesus Christ? If you do, celebrate that special person. If you do not, find someone. A pastor, a Bible study leader, a member of your congregation. Another challenge is for *you* to become that person in someone's life.

_____

_____

_____

_____

_____

_____

_____

_____

_____

_____

_____

Philippians 3:4–21

Paul makes it sound so easy. But it really is just that simple. Focus 100 percent on Christ Jesus. Try to mirror his life on earth, and long for the day he returns to take us to live with him in heaven, when your weak mortal body will change into a glorious body like his own. The beautiful thing is that no matter what flaws you see today in your body, Christ looks at you as if you are perfect, with a beautiful, glorious body. You *are* beautiful!

Philippians 4:1–23

Paul shares so much wisdom with you today. One of my favorites is verse 6, which I'm going to post on my daughter, Hannah's, backpack as soon as I finish here: "Don't worry about anything, instead pray about everything." Wow! Also, verse 8: "Fix your thoughts on what is true and honorable and right. Think about things that are pure and lovely and admirable." Think about things that are excellent and worthy of praise. What do you have in your life today that is worthy of praise? Well, then, praise the Lord for that!

Colossians 1:1–17

What a beautiful prayer Paul has for the Colossians. My prayer for you today is the same prayer Paul had for the Colossians all those years ago: "May God give you the complete understanding of what he wants to do in your lives, and I ask him to make you wise with spiritual wisdom." Amen.

Colossians 1:18–2:7

You are growing in Christ every day. Your roots should be growing deeper and deeper so no one can topple you, so you are not uprooted by a slight breeze. If you concentrate too much on the pretty foliage and the parts of you that people see, you'll become top-heavy, and the slightest breeze will uproot you. No, instead concentrate on building strong roots in Christ so you stand strong for him!

Colossians 2:8–23

Don't judge others. Stay humble, and stay connected to Christ Jesus. All other worldly disciplines are meaningless without Christ. He needs to be your center focus of life.

Colossians 3:1–17

I admit I like clothes and looking nice. So when Paul instructs the Colossians on how to clothe themselves, I sit up and take notice. He didn't mention the importance of wearing any name-brand clothes. Just imagine how beautiful you'll be when you cloth yourself with tenderhearted mercy, kindness, humility, gentleness, and patience. Then, over all of that, you put on your coat of love—your most important piece of clothing! Love that binds us in perfect harmony.

Colossians 3:18–4:18

If you ever become frustrated with your job or school, go to verses 23–24: "Work hard, cheerfully as if you were working for the Lord rather than people. Serve your master with a joyful heart." You have no idea how God is working through you at your job and school in order to touch the lives of those around you. Stay positive in whatever you do.

1 Thessalonians 1:1–2:8

"We always thank God for all of you, and pray for you constantly." That's how I feel about you. It's how Paul feels about the church in Thessalonica. Never underestimate the power of prayer. God is listening. Talk to him. Also talk to others about Jesus. You never know how the Holy Spirit will work through your life. Plant the seed every chance you get.

1 Thessalonians 2:9–3:13

"Night and day we toil." Being a Christian and spreading the Good News of Jesus Christ is not for wimps. It takes hard work, long days, and rejection from the world. But take heart—the reward of a personal relationship with Jesus far outweighs any amount of work.

1 Thessalonians 4:1–5:3

What a beautiful scene. I so look forward to that day when we meet up with Jesus in the clouds to live with him forever. Oh, what a glorious day that will be. "This should be your ambition! To live a quiet life, minding your own business and working with your hands."

1 Thessalonians 5:4–28

Encourage your pastor and others who have been called to a life of work for Christ Jesus. Pray for them and their spouses. Pray on their behalf for wisdom and strength to continue their work. They're human, but they've been called to do superhuman jobs.

2 Thessalonians 1:1–12

I pray God will make you worthy of the life to which he called you.
What has God called you to do? To love others unconditionally, to
share the Good News, to teach, to preach, to heal. I praise God
that he has specially made you to be unique. May God, by his
power, fulfill all your good intentions and faithful deeds.

2 Thessalonians 2:1–17

Stand firm. Be strong. Don't waver in your faith. You'll be tested.
You'll be lied to. Pray for yourself and for other Christians.
Know there's nothing too strong for your God!

_____

_____

_____

_____

_____

_____

_____

_____

_____

_____

_____

_____

_____

_____

DAY 287

2 Thessalonians 3:1–18

Don't be afraid of hard work. Instead be thankful for it. Go above and beyond what is asked of you. Work day and night. Idle minds lead to trouble. So keep your body and mind productive. There's always another person you can help. Who and how will you help today?

1 Timothy 1:1–20

How amazing would it be to have a friend filled with the love that
comes from pure heart, a clear conscience, and sincere faith?
That sounds like the perfect friend. You can be that friend
to someone.

_____

_____

_____

_____

_____

_____

_____

_____

_____

_____

_____

_____

DAY 289

1 Timothy 2:1–15

What makes you attractive? Is it your flashy clothes, jewelry, makeup, or hair Or is it the good things you do and the good person you are? It's okay to take pride in your appearance. Just be careful that your outward appearance doesn't become your number one priority. It's far more important to be beautiful on the inside than on the outside.

_____

_____

_____

_____

_____

_____

_____

_____

_____

_____

_____

_____

1 Timothy 3:1–16

Paul describes what it takes to become an elder or deacon in the church. Some churches use other terminology for their church leaders. But all leaders should have the character traits Paul describes. Do you have what it takes to be a leader in your church and family? What areas in your life need improvement to make you worthy of leading Christ Jesus's church?

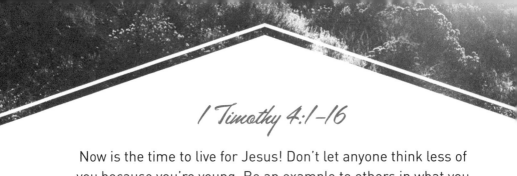

1 Timothy 4:1–16

Now is the time to live for Jesus! Don't let anyone think less of you because you're young. Be an example to others in what you teach, in the way you live your life, and in your love, your faith, and your purity. Others are watching. Let Jesus shine through you in all you do and say.

1 Timothy 5:1–25

There are a few lessons in today's reading. First lesson: In love, take care of your family and treat older people with respect. Second lesson: Do not judge others. Only God knows what's in their hearts and the things they have done, good or bad. It's your job to love unconditionally. Leave the judging to God!

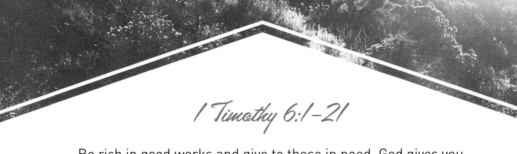

1 Timothy 6:1–21

Be rich in good works and give to those in need. God gives you all you need for your enjoyment. True religion with contentment is great wealth. Thank you, Lord, for all you have blessed me with. You know my needs. Help me be content. Amen.

2 Timothy 1:1–18

It's hard to leave and say good-bye to someone you love. There are often tears. Even Paul and Timothy cried when they had to leave one another. But, oh, the joy and anticipation when you see that loved one again! Just imagine the joy when you actually see Jesus face-to-face! Oh, what a day that will be!

2 Timothy 2:1–21

The word of God cannot be chained. There's so much wisdom and direction for your life in God's word. Read it, and then reread it, and then read it again. And all the while, live by it. The word of God cannot be chained.

2 Timothy 2:22–3:17

Run from anything that stimulates youthful lust. Grow in your
faith. Learn and gain wisdom from reading the scripture,
which is inspired by God. You're never too old to stop learning,
and you'll learn something new every time you read God's word.
He will continue revealing more and more of himself to you,
and you will grow closer to him.

2 Timothy 4:1–22

It's important to have fellow Christians for support. You can't grow in your faith or help others grow in theirs if you isolate yourself. Don't fool yourself into thinking you don't need a faith family. You need a community of believers. If you don't have that support now, pray that God puts those people in your life. Who's on your Jesus team?

Titus 1:1–16

Live a godly life. What you do and how you live say much more about you than what you say. Model your life to be like an elder. Everything is pure to those whose hearts are pure.

Titus 2:1–15

You should live in this evil world with self-control, right conduct, and devotion to God. Be a positive role model for those younger than you. Teach them about the love of Jesus. Be the Bible to those who haven't read it. Encourage them to explore the life and teachings of Jesus.

DAY 300

Titus 3:1–15

God has generously poured out the Holy Spirit on you through Jesus. Not because of anything you have done, but because of his mercy and love for you—unconditional, all-encompassing love for you. Soak it in, and feel his loving embrace.

Philemon 1–25

What do you trust the Lord with? What do you hold back from him? Is there something or someone in your life you just can't let go of? Pray on it. Take the leap. Trust Jesus with all things. He gave all for you. Are you willing to do the same for him?

Hebrews 1:1–14

There's a special bond between a parent and child.
God is Jesus's Father and your Father. He loves you unconditionally. He loves you so much that he sent Jesus to earth to
save you, so that you can live with him forever in heaven.
Thank Jesus for dying so that you may live.

Hebrews 2:1–18

You know you have a Heavenly Father. But you also have brothers and sisters in Christ Jesus! You have a faith family here on earth, who will also spend eternity with you in heaven. Is there anyone you know who's not part of your faith family? Show them Jesus's love, and invite them to be one of God's children.

Hebrews 3:1–19

Today you must listen to his voice. In what way do you listen to God's voice? By reading God's word in the Bible, by devotion, by prayer, by quiet time alone with him? Life on earth gets busy with all sorts of noise and tasks. Remember to take time daily to listen to his voice.

_____

_____

_____

_____

_____

_____

_____

_____

_____

_____

_____

_____

Hebrews 4:1–16

Earlier we talked about the importance of working hard.
Today you learn about your reward for hard work—*rest*!
When all is said and done, and you are exhausted, you can fall into
God's arms and rest.

Hebrews 5:1–14

Even Jesus learned through suffering. God has a plan for your life. Parts of that plan will include suffering and trials. God is molding you into the person he created you to be. Do not continue to drink milk your entire life. Grow. Sink your teeth into the meat of the scriptures.

Hebrews 6:1–20

God has made a promise and oath to you. Sometimes life here on earth stinks. It's not easy. There's a lot of sin out there. But you are meant for better things that come with salvation. God is not unfair. He has great things in store for you. Trust him! Hold onto his promise with confidence. It's impossible for God to lie.

Hebrews 7:1–17

Melchizedek: king of justice, king of peace. There's no history of ancestors before him, and he seemed to live forever. Melchizedek blessed Abraham. Abraham gave Melchizedek 10 percent of all he had won in battle. Do you see any similarities? This is what the psalmist said about Christ: "You are a priest forever in the line of Melchizedek."

Hebrews 7:18–28

Jesus is your high priest. He will never die or leave you. He pleads with God on your behalf daily. He is perfect and knows no limitations. He is your rock and your salvation always and forever.

DAY 310

Hebrews 8:1–13

Thank you, God, for your new covenant to your people. For sending your Son, Jesus Christ, and the Holy Spirit to live within us. Thank you for your forgiveness. You are a caring, loving God.

_____

_____

_____

_____

_____

_____

_____

_____

_____

_____

_____

_____

_____

Hebrews 9:1-10

What an elaborate setting. It was only a tent, but its contents were over-the-top extravagant. There were so many rules. I'm thankful that today all people are welcome to come into the inner room. We're welcome not only once a year, but at any time. Christ's blood was shed for the sacrifice of allowing you full access to the inner room.

_____

_____

_____

_____

_____

_____

_____

_____

_____

_____

_____

DAY 312

Hebrew 9:11–28

Jesus—the sacrificial Lamb, who came to earth as a sacrifice for your sins. He cares for you that much. He came to save you once and for always. His blood covers the tent of the entire earth. Someday he is coming back to take you to heaven to live with him there. I wait eagerly for that day.

_____

_____

_____

_____

_____

_____

_____

_____

_____

_____

Hebrews 10:1-17

Christ died one time. He died only once and for always. You come to Christ once, and you are with him always. We celebrate Christmas and Easter to remember the sacrifice Jesus made for you and me. We celebrate out of love, not out of commitment to laws.

_____

_____

_____

_____

_____

_____

_____

_____

_____

_____

_____

DAY 314

Hebrews 10:18–39

Go ahead—walk right into the presence of God with a true heart, fully trusting in him. You're an open book. You can't hide from him. God knows everything about you, and he still loves you unconditionally. Take all your fears and insecurities and lay them at Jesus's feet. God will take care of you.
You are loved.

DAY 315

Hebrews 11:1–16

Do you have faith? What is your hope? Take time to read the Old Testament stories. Soak in the history. Sincerely seek God. Have the confident assurance that what you hope for will happen. Faith is the evidence of things you cannot yet see. Keep looking forward, toward your heavenly homeland.

Hebrews 11:17–31

How strong is your faith? The Bible is chock-full of examples of faithful men and women. Will you be the faithful example to students in your school, people in your neighborhood, coworkers, or even members of your church? Take a stand. Let your faith show to everyone you meet.

Hebrews 11:32–12:13

What is weighing you down? What sins are slowing down your progress? Now is the time to remove those sins from your life. It'll make you stronger and give you more endurance to run the race for Christ. Your body may become tired, but finish strong! Your reward waits for you just across the finish line.

Hebrews 12:14–29

Once again you are instructed to love one another. Live in peace with everyone, and watch out for each other. You're not meant to live alone but to live in community where you care for one another. Let us be thankful and please God by worshiping him with holy fear and awe. For our God is a consuming fire.

_____

_____

_____

_____

_____

_____

_____

_____

_____

_____

_____

Hebrews 13:1–25

I love the thought of entertaining angels and not even knowing it! I think back on all the people who have come and gone in and out of our home. I know some of those people have been angels. I have been blessed by being in their presence. Entertain angels in your home. Show hospitality to strangers.

James 1:1–18

Do you have any trouble in your life today? Praise God for your trouble. For when your faith is tested, your endurance has a chance to grow. And when your endurance is fully developed, you'll be strong in character and ready for anything.

_____

_____

_____

_____

_____

_____

_____

_____

_____

_____

_____

_____

_____

_____

_____

DAY 321

James 1:19–2:17

Words of wisdom: "Be quick to listen, slow to speak, and slow
to get angry." Help those in need. Look around you today to see
what you can do to help someone. Who's hungry? Who's cold?
Faith that doesn't show itself by good deeds is no faith at all;
it's dead and useless.

James 2:18–3:18

Your faith is made complete by the things you do. Faith is dead without doing good for others. The tongue is such a small part of the body, but it can do so much damage or so much good, depending on how you choose to use it. Be wise. Control your tongue, and strive to be a peacemaker.

James 4:1–17

Things. They are only things. Don't waste your time lusting over things. Once you acquire them, you'll only be disappointed. Things will not make you happy. True happiness and contentment can only be found through Jesus and pouring his love out onto others.

_____

_____

_____

_____

_____

_____

_____

_____

_____

_____

_____

James 5:1-20

Where are you storing your treasure? On earth or in heaven? Be patient and know that the trouble you're going through will only last for a season. God's timing is perfect. Trust him and the plan he has for you.

1 Peter 1:1–12

All currency in the United States is backed by gold before it can go into circulation. Dollars are nothing without gold to back it up. Gold is a precious metal. Still, your faith is far more precious to God than mere gold. You are far more valuable than any amount of money or precious metal. You are priceless in God's eye—and in mine.

_____

_____

_____

_____

_____

_____

_____

_____

_____

_____

_____

_____

_____

DAY 326

1 Peter 1:13–2:10

Jesus is the living cornerstone of God's temple. He is the foundation that holds everything and everyone together. Cling to that strong rock.

1 Peter 2:11–3:7

Keep away from evil desires. What desires do you have? Are they evil, or are they godly desires? If they're evil or desires of this world, reject them. Turn your back to them, and move forward. And when you're married, honor your spouse. Treat your spouse with love and respect. The two of you will be partners, and life is so much easier when you work together.

_____

_____

_____

_____

_____

_____

_____

_____

_____

_____

_____

_____

1 Peter 3:8–4:6

Who can you pay back with a blessing today? When people are mean, unfair, or unkind to you, don't retaliate. Instead pay them back with a blessing. That will make them stop and think, "What's up with that guy (or gal)?" Have a tender heart, full of love for everyone.

1 Peter 4:7–5:14

Be earnest and disciplined in your prayers. How much time do you spend talking to God? Give all your worries and cares to God, for he cares about what happens to you. He is available twenty-four hours a day, seven days a week. He is waiting to hear from you. Tell him about the best and worst part of your day. Talk to him.

2 Peter 1:1–21

How has your live changed by knowing Jesus better and better? As you draw nearer to him and your faith grows, do you see changes in your priorities? Your faith will produce a life of moral excellence. Which leads to knowing God better. Which leads to self-control. Which leads to patient endurance. Which leads to godliness. Which leads to love for other Christians. Which ultimately leads to genuine love for everyone!

2 Peter 2:1-22

You're a slave to whatever controls you. Oh, be careful and watch for those who try to deceive you. Many out there are chasing after their own desires. They'll do whatever it takes for you to go along with them. Stay grounded in God's will. Turn your back to the deceivers. Follow Jesus. Spend extra time in prayer and his word.

2 Peter 3:1–18

The Lord is being patient for your sake. He wants you to do the right thing. He wants you to live with him forever. He wants you to tell your friends about Jesus so we can all live in heaven together. What an amazing time that will be. A world filled with Christians praising Jesus's name!

1 John 1:1-10

God will forgive you of your sins. There are no sins too big for God. Go to him and confess them all. He will forgive you. What a freeing feeling to know all your sins have been washed away with Christ's blood and forgotten forever. Put your sins behind you. Get busy living in the light for the Lord.

1 John 2:1–17

Are you living in God? Do you obey his word and really love him? Or do you lust over everything you see and take great pride in your possessions? These things will all fade away. The only thing that will last is *love*. Your love for others and your love for the Lord. Let Christ's love show through the way you interact with others.

_____

_____

_____

_____

_____

_____

_____

_____

_____

_____

_____

_____

1 John 2:18–3:6

You are God's child! No matter how old you are, you'll always be God's child! Keep watch for the Antichrist. He won't show up at your door with a cape and red horns. No, he'll show up promising everything you have ever desired. Don't fall for his antics. Instead draw close to your Heavenly Father.

1 John 3:7–24

Our message today is again to love others. But today you're told that *saying* you love others is not enough. You need to love others through your actions. Anyone can say, "I love you." But it takes someone with a heart for Jesus to *live* love for others.

_____

_____

_____

_____

_____

_____

_____

_____

_____

_____

_____

_____

_____

1 John 4:1-21

God is love! As you live in God, your love grows more perfect. How beautiful is that? You cannot out-give or out-love God. The more you give, the more love grows. So don't hold back. Love up on someone today. What are some examples of ways you can show love to others?

1 John 5:1–21

God does not ask you to live your Christian life alone. No, quite the contrary. His desire is for you to live in community with other believers. To support one another in all things. Keep away from anything (bad or good) that might take God's place in your heart. Nothing should outweigh God for that number one priority in your heart.

2 John 1–13

Today John is writing a letter to the church and its members. He has an important message to share with them: to love one another. He has more to talk about, but he wants to do it face-to-face. In today's world, so much communication happens through e-mails, texts, and other social media, which is fine. But it's also important to turn off the electronics and sit down with one another to talk. Take the time today to seek out someone to visit face-to-face. Oh, and remember to do some listening too!

3 John 1–15

I agree with John: there is no greater joy than your children living in the truth. God has given you wonderful, unique talents, just as he has given them to my own children. It does my heart well to see young people using those gifts to the best of your ability to do the will of God. There's no greater joy for your parents or your Heavenly Father.

Jude 1–25

Don't live like an animal that does whatever its instincts tells it. Instead live with purpose so God's love can bless you as you wait for the eternal life our Lord Jesus Christ, in his mercy, will give you. Live for Jesus, and he will bless you today.

_____

_____

_____

_____

_____

_____

_____

_____

_____

_____

_____

_____

_____

Revelation 1:1–20

You have made it to the homestretch! Today you begin your last and most controversial book in the Bible—Revelation. Jesus has moved from the baby born in a manger, to Jesus the teacher, to Jesus on the cross, to Jesus our Heavenly Father. The Alpha and the Omega. The Beginning and the End. The one who is, who always was, and who is still to come. The almighty one. No matter how things change, Jesus is constant.

Revelation 2:1–17

Jesus addressed three of the seven churches in today's reading. He told each of them to listen to the Spirit and understand what the Spirit is saying to them. There's so much noise in our lives today. Find a quiet spot, and listen to what the Holy Spirit has to say to you today. Don't rush it. Spend a little quiet time with the Spirit.

Revelation 2:18–3:6

God is watching you, just as he was watching the churches. How does that make you feel? Would God be pleased with your choices, or would he be disappointed? Anyone who's willing to hear should listen to the Spirit and understand what the Spirit is saying to the churches and to you.

_____

_____

_____

_____

_____

_____

_____

_____

_____

_____

_____

_____

Revelation 3:7–22

If you have the love of Jesus in your heart, it's impossible to be a "lukewarm" Christian. Let your passion be seen. Become that pillar in the temple of God! You're only on this earth for a short time. So make the most of it!

Revelation 4:1–11

What a scene. Amazing. Beautiful. Fabulous. These heavenly beings and elders spend all of their time, day after day and night after night, praising God. You should be doing the same with a song in your heart praising your Lord God. Holy, holy, holy is the Lord God Almighty. The one who always was, who is, and who is still to come! Alleluia. Amen.

Revelation 5:1–14

The Lamb who was slain, Jesus, is the only one able to open the sealed scroll. He has paid the price. And when he takes the scroll, the four beings hold out gold bowls to him filled with incense. The prayers of God's people—your prayers, my prayers—are being presented to Jesus. You're not in this race alone. You're surrounded by love and support here on earth and in heaven.

Revelation 6:1–17

Wars, world hunger, diseases, cancer, earthquakes are all
around us. But even as these terrible things unfold,
remember the Lamb, Jesus, is still in control.
Put all of your trust in him.

Revelation 7:1-17

Has your robe been washed in the blood of the Lamb and made white? Do you stand in front of the throne of God, praising him day and night? If you do, you'll never be hungry or thirsty again. He will shelter you and wipe away your tears. So be happy and praise the Lamb of God.

Revelation 8:1–13

Talking about "the end days" or dying can be a scary thing. But you do not need to fear death. Instead celebrate it. Because that is when you'll get to see Jesus and live with him forever. You'll get to be one of the angels falling at the foot of the throne to worship him.

Revelation 9:1-21

Our God is a just God. You'll be held accountable. So stay away from evil. Stay away from witchcraft. Do not worship idols of gold, silver, bronze, stone, or wood. There's only one worthy of all your praise. Give all you have to God the Father.

Revelation 10:1–11

God has a mysterious plan that will be fulfilled. You're viewing only glimpses of what heaven and the end days will be like. You can't comprehend the magnitude of God's plan. You move forward by faith, knowing that God lives forever and ever. He created heaven and everything in it, the earth and everything in it, and the sea and everything in it.

Revelation 11:1-19

God has planned every detail. From the beginning of time, until today, until the end of time. God has a plan. He had a plan for Adam and Eve. He had a plan for his Son, Jesus. He has a plan for the seven angels and the twenty-four elders. And he has a plan for you and for me. Follow him!

_____

_____

_____

_____

_____

_____

_____

_____

_____

Revelation 12:1–17

Satan is very smart and very clever. Be careful of his manipulating ways. There's only one way to concur Satan. By the blood of the Lamb. Don't be deceived by his cunning ways. Stay rooted in God's word. Wash yourself daily in the blood. He will protect you from the evil one.

Revelation 12:18–13:18

Pray for wisdom. The end times will be difficult.
The days we live in now are difficult. Do not be swayed
by things of this world. Or by 666–Satan. Instead stay strong.
Find comfort in the love of Jesus.

Revelation 14:1-20

The scene in heaven continues to grow toward the climax when Jesus calls you to live forever with him. The message has not changed. Keep your focus on Jesus and not on the things of this earth. Let God's holy people endure persecution patiently, and remain firm to the end, obeying his commands and trusting in Jesus.

Revelation 15:1-8

I want to be one of those victorious people in heaven
with a harp, singing, praising God. Will you join me?
"Great and marvelous are your actions, Lord God Almighty."

_____

_____

_____

_____

_____

_____

_____

_____

_____

_____

_____

_____

_____

Revelation 16:1–21

God is a just God. He will send his wrath upon the earth. How do you handle trial and tribulation? When you're faced with trage-dy, do you curse God's name, or do you praise his name? Do you pull away from God, or do you draw near to him? I pray that no matter how bad things are in your life, you'll always find comfort and peace in your Lord Jesus Christ.

Revelation 17:1–18

The evil in this world comes in many forms. There's so much corruption everywhere. It's easy to be distracted by all this evil. No matter how many people, cities, or armies battle against God, they will fail. The Lamb is Lord over all lords and King over all kings. His people are called chosen and faithful ones. Remain one of God's chosen and faithful children.

Revelation 18:1–24

In an instant, a whole city is gone. Think of tornadoes, tsunamis, and the Twin Towers in New York. All tragic, but all small compared to Babylon. Gold, silver, jewels, pearls, fine linens, purple dye, silks, scarlet cloths, every kind of perfumed wood, ivory goods, objects made of expensive wood, bronze, iron, marble, cinnamon, spices, incense, myrrh, frankincense, wine, olive oil, fine flour, wheat, cattle, sheep, horses, chariots, and slaves—all gone in an instant. So in the end, how valuable were any of those things?

Revelation 19:1-21

Hallelujah! I love all the imagery in today's passage. After all the pain and suffering, God rides in on his white horse to kill all the evil forever. Let us be glad and rejoice and honor him. Blessed are those who are invited to the wedding feast of the Lamb. The fine linen robe dipped in blood. "On his robe and thigh was written 'King of kings and Lord of lords.'"

Revelation 20:1–15

Those who have been persecuted for Jesus's sake will have their day. And what a glorious day that will be! We will all be held accountable for how we lived our lives. Did you give more than you took? Did you make the world a better place by being in it? It's not too late to start. Who can you comfort today?

Revelation 21:1-27

"It is finished!" What a glorious, amazing, fabulous, incredible place. No more sadness. No more pain. No more fear. Only God, the Alpha and the Omega, the Beginning and the End. To all who are thirsty, God will give the springs of the water of life. All who are victorious will inherit all of these blessings. Our heavenly home! I'm going to live there with you and our Heavenly Father.

Revelation 22:1–21

Be ready. Don't stand outside the gates as one who loves to live a lie. Be true to yourself. Be true to God. Be ready because he is coming soon. Amen! Come, Lord Jesus!

Favorite Verses

Favorite Verses

Favorite Verses

Congratulations—you did it! You made it from Matthew 1:1 to Revelation 22:21. I'm so proud of you. You have learned. You have grown in your faith. Continue your journey. Let the love of Christ Jesus flow freely from you onto others. Thanks for spending your year with me and Jesus and for walking in the word!

Love,

Wanda

About the Author

Wanda Playter was the youth director at Emman-uel Reformed Church in Wisconsin. Later, she be-came the youth board chairman at Salem Lutheran Church in Iowa. Wanda has always had a passion for youth and Jesus. She was born and raised in the Midwest, married her high school sweetheart, and has three amazing children.

She does not have an English degree and did not set out to write a book. She started writing to her children but felt God calling, and the more she said "No, I'm not qualified—choose someone else," the more God pushed. So here she is, with her first book published. She is over-the-moon excited to share it with you and your families.

For more information on Wanda and her book, visit WandaPlayter.com.